EARTH'S GOLDEN AGE

Life beyond 2012

A Matthew Book

with Suzanne Ward

ISBN 9780971787506

MATTHEW BOOKS
P. O. Box 1043
Camas, Washington 98607

www.matthewbooks.com
suzy@matthewbooks.com

Printed in the United States

Cover design by Hartmut Jager

DEDICATION

With unconditional love to our family on Earth
from your brothers and sisters in other worlds

The power of LOVE is the key to the Golden Age

EARTH'S GOLDEN AGE

Life beyond 2012

CONTENTS

Earth's Golden Age

Prelude

Greetings, my beloved children. This is God speaking. I say God because that is how my scribe Suzy knows me—whatever name you call me is fine, I answer to all of them. I answer all your questions and prayers too, and I wish more of you understood how that goes—in time you will.

You may—or may not—be astounded to know that before you were born, you chose to be exactly the person you are as well as your role in helping to bring a glorious new world to Earth's doorstep.

You don't remember doing that, so I'll tell you about it. A few of you signed on to be in the vanguard, others decided to actively support those way-showers, and most of you chose to live in the godly ways that spread light to everyone. And what a magnificent collective accomplishment—*Earth's Golden Age!*

It was from me that the inspiration came for this name. It describes the brilliance of the light from you and many, many of my other children. That light boosted Earth out of the darkness that far too long had wreaked havoc and devastation on the planet.

Light, which is very same energy as love, is the most powerful force in the cosmos. This energy is the pure essence of Creator, and it's what you and I and all other souls throughout the cosmos are made of—it's our Beginnings as eternal souls. As enormous as our universe is, it's not the only one—at this moment, there are six others.

Anyway, getting away from that darkness is why
Earth is ascending, and this is going to bring about some
huge differences in your world. Many of you still are
adjusting to the changes so far. At the same time you're
thinking that just maybe they portend a "better world,"
you are wondering *but what's coming next!?* with a tad of
trepidation. Some of you have a *lot* of it.

I can tell you in a nut shell what's coming next—
peace, harmony and unity of Spirit! But—I am you and
you are me, so I know you want the *what, why* and *how*
and *who* of it all. Frankly, I'd be disappointed if you
didn't want to know because this is my little book with
the answers.

As I speak, plans are afoot for my children whom you
call "extraterrestrials" to introduce themselves. Some
are living among you undetected and some are living
inside the planet—they're all "terrestrials." The actual
extraterrestrials—you'll get over that impersonal way of
thinking about them—will be landing their crafts that
have been circling in your skies for ages and still others
have been helping you from so far away that you can't
imagine it.

They are among the "advanced" ones of my very
sizable flock. Their light, and their technologies too,
have been helping Gaia's planetary body—you call it
Earth—all along its ascension route. They've also been
helping you move upward and onward consciously and
spiritually.

You need to become acquainted with some of these
brothers and sisters of yours. Without their help, who
knows where you'd be today? Well, yes, I would know,
but that's another story.

Now, my beloveds, read on...

Preface

It was the middle of June 2012 when God said, *"Little Suzy, I want you to consider publishing a short but vital book with the title* Earth's Golden Age—Life beyond 2012.*"* Then He told me what should be in it.

My reply—*I don't think a book like that is necessary because the information is in many of Matthew's 150 messages on my Web site and scattered around in three of the books*—handed God his rebuttal on a silver platter. "Exactly! *It's here and there and here and there and it all needs to be in ONE place!"*

After a few days of wondering how I could possibly find time for all the tasks involved in publishing a book, I said, "Okay, God" and He said, *"Let's get started!"*

In accordance with His directions, Matthew covers Earth's history and ascension, the range of extraterrestrial assistance, and life in the Golden Age; and representatives of other worlds describe themselves and how they're helping us.

As God mentioned, He wants us to know about our universal family. His other reason for wanting this book is *"so all of my beloved children on Earth can feel excited and joyous about everything that lies ahead!"*

Suzanne Ward
August 2012

2012 and Earth's Ascension

History

In the continuum, where what you think of as past, present and future actually are a series of events happening simultaneously, the beginning and also the completion of Earth's ascension are *fait accompli*, so you could say that both "times" have been known for untold ages. The same can be said about the conditions that led to Earth's choice to leave third density when the alignment of celestial bodies opens a window of opportunity around the end of your calendar year 2012.

Often density and dimension are used interchangeably as if they are synonymous, and in a universal context, they aren't. Everything has dimensions—width, length, height, weight, volume—whereas density has narrowly defined scientific applications.

The Mayan calendar stops at December 21, 2012 because that is the end of a 26,000-year linear cycle. At this point in each cycle, the planetary juxtaposition in your solar system produces especially powerful energy surges that present a propitious time for Earth to exit third density, where darkness thrives, and move into fourth, where the low vibrations of darkness cannot enter.

Previous cycles came and went because Earth was too weak to move out of deep third density where she was mired by the darkness that controlled life on the planet. Her successive populations had become brutal in their treatment of each other, and eons of bloodshed had amassed such an amount of negativity that Earth reached death throes.

Twice she saved herself by initiating cataclysmic events that released the negativity, but those also destroyed all life on the planet and that caused her deep sorrow. She did not want to repeat those traumatic episodes and that is why she cried out for help.

Instantly God authorized civilizations to provide the lifesaving assistance Earth needed. They beamed massive amounts of light to start stabilizing her orbit, which had become so erratic that she was on the brink of flying out into space and certain destruction, and to help her jar loose from deep third density.

The light that enabled the planet's survival and started it on its ascension course also served to enlighten Earth's human residents so they could make conscious choices in keeping with her vision of a Golden Age—a peaceful, healthy world where all peoples live in harmony with each other and all of Nature. The world she envisioned would be a return to her beginnings as the pristine, beauteous paradise you know as Eden.

In linear time, Earth's cry for help and the beginning of her ascension process was at the end of your 1930s, but the ascension plan had long been in operation. Members of galactic and intergalactic federations had sought counsel of the highest beings in this universe, and out of discussions at that topmost level, a master plan was developed for Earth's ascension and her Golden Age.

Only in the timelessness of the continuum could the countless complexities of manifesting Earth's vision into reality be intricately planned and executed. It required the matching-up of the many billions of souls who clamored to participate and inviting souls from highly spiritually and intellectually evolved civilizations to be the leaders and way-showers.

Foremost considerations were that Creator's cosmic law of free will with its inseparable powers of manifestation had to be honored, and because the world Earth desired would be co-created *for* and *by* her residents, it would have to be according to what they—*you!*—desire and envision.

Each person manifests the circumstances of his or her life, and in combination, those manifestations make up the world. So it was essential that enough of the collective minds would become enlightened, inspired and dedicated to co-creating the Golden Age of Earth's vision.

Of paramount importance was the need to accommodate the majority of souls, those who wanted to attain balance by completing the third density karma they had incurred in multiple lifetimes on Earth and various other places in the universe. The master plan had to include circumstances whereby they could complete their karma in one lifetime and thus move forward with Earth into fourth density.

Karma is neither a reward for "being good" nor a punishment for "being bad." Karma is the form of divine grace that provides each soul as many opportunities as necessary to achieve the balanced experiencing that leads to the spiritual and intellectual progress that is every soul's goal.

Eager to take advantage of this unprecedented one-lifetime opportunity, souls chose whatever circumstances they needed. The majority required experiencing one or more of these conditions: impoverishment, cruel oppression, slavery, starvation, war or other violence, grief, disease, physical or mental debilities or incapacitation, legal injustices, severe discord in relationships, very short life span. What is regarded as sad or tragic lives or lives cut far too short are those souls' *free will choices*, and some strong souls volunteered to comply with the choices by causing suffering, hardships, grief, death and disharmony.

Knowing all the ramifications of the master plan, and because soul contracts are made with unconditional love and are designed for all participants' spiritual growth, many more souls than could inhabit the planet during the ascension decades wanted to incarnate. Those whom the highest universal council did not select would contribute to the ascension process in other vital ways, and those who were selected enthusiastically looked forward to filling the roles that would let them evolve themselves at the same time they were assisting others to do so.

In short, *prior to birth* all peoples now on the planet and the many who left during the past several years knew exactly what they and all others had chosen to experience and why. All were born with that knowledge, but it soon was forgotten as they adjusted to "life in the flesh" and its needs, and even more so, indoctrination by family, educators, religions, society and governments.

However, the master planners knew that would happen because it is inherent in third density world inhabitants. Therefore, it was arranged that light in ever-increasing abundance would be supplied by beings throughout the universe to merge Earth peoples' consciousness with their soul level knowingness.

Now let us go back to ascension in your linear time. The parameters of the celestial window between third and fourth densities have a degree of flexibility, so the planet's entry into fourth doesn't have to occur December 21, 2012, or any other specific date in the same narrow timeframe, but that doesn't lessen one iota the validity of the Mayans' calculation. They were closely aligned with members of advanced civilizations who were on the planet then to share their knowledge and manifesting skills, and they gave the Mayans that date. They knew it because Earth's ascension—*its scope and speed is unique in this universe!*—already was a done deal in the continuum. What you call time actually is *energy*, and what you are sensing as time passing faster and faster is the effect of Earth's ascension through increasingly lighter energy planes on her way to fourth density.

There are differing opinions about which density you're in right now, and no wonder. By our numbering densities to indicate advancement, it does sound as if one part of space comes to an abrupt edge and at that point another begins, and that isn't so. There is no finite demarcation between densities—the flow of energy cannot be sharply divided or compartmentalized. As Earth ascends through the "last" wafting energy streamers of third density, which comingle with the "first" streamers of fourth, you won't notice a dynamic difference from one day to the next. There will be no ribbon-cutting ceremony, so to say.

The confusion about density is compounded because the word has two definitions. One is *mass* or the *location of a mass* as distinguished from your idea of discarnate—without any mass or form—which is how you think of souls in spirit. You can't see us even when we are standing beside you because our etheric bodies vibrate at frequencies that third density vision cannot detect, just as you cannot see blades of a fan that is whirring on its highest setting. But indeed etheric bodies have a degree of mass, and it lessens in density as souls continue to evolve spiritually.

And that brings us to the other meaning of density, which denotes the status of a soul's *spiritual evolution*. As I explain both densities in the context of your homeland planet and its populations through the ages, please remember that it is a civilization's collective thoughts, feelings and actions that manifest the state of their world.

Earth's *mass* started spiraling from its original home in fifth density because negativity was increasing in the collective consciousness of her ancient civilizations. The planet's descent continued in accordance with the inhabitants' reduced *evolutionary status* as more and more darkness entered their thoughts, motives and deeds, and eventually the planet reached deep third density in *mass* and *location* because the population's *spiritual status* had reached that low density.

The two episodes of negativity release in those times so long ago had saved the life of the planet, but its weakened condition kept it rooted in third density *mass* and *location*. However, throughout the eons that the planet and the collective consciousness of successive populations were mired in that low density, Gaia, Earth's soul, retained its fifth density *evolvement status*. During those long ages when the peoples were third density in body mass and soul evolvement status, a few highly evolved souls were born into their midst—God's messengers and the occasional visionary philosopher, scientist, naturalist or artist.

At this juncture in Earth's ascension—midway in 2012—her planetary body has reached high third density in mass and location in its galaxy. While the bodies of many of her residents also are at that density mass-wise, bodies of persons who have embraced the light have evolved from third density's carbon-based cellular structure into the crystalline form that enables both consciousness-raising and physical survival in fourth and higher densities. During the past two decades or so, advanced souls have embodied with crystalline cellular makeup.

In *spiritual evolution,* Earth's population ranges from third density to seventh, and a few have *de*volved to second or first due to the darkness of their free will choices and their persistence in consciously refusing the intense light that is constantly beamed to them. Among them are some of the individuals who volunteered to play the heaviest roles to give the majority souls the opportunity to complete their third density karma.

The agreement was, when that point was reached— and it was about ten years ago in your counting—those individuals would join the light forces. However, they had become so captivated with controlling the masses through oppression, fear, corruption, deception and greed that they refused to give up their power or their illegally-gained vast fortunes. The light they had at birth diminished to only the spark that is their life force, and because they continued their unconscionable activities, darkness remained on the planet.

These people call themselves the Illuminati, which means "the enlightened," but they don't publicly refer to themselves by that name. Working in secret, they are in such disparate areas as governments and regulatory bodies; national and international economies, banking and commerce; royal families; the United Nations; law, policing and justice systems; educational institutions and church hierarchies; media and entertainment venues; the Zionist movement and multinational corporations. In short, the Illuminati have been influencing or controlling everything that affects life in your world.

Almost all souls who incarnated to complete third density karma by being lightworkers—persons whose activities and behavior radiate light that benefits not only themselves, but can uplift all the lives that are touched by their light—have attained fourth density *soul evolvement* and their cells are changing into the crystalline of fourth density *mass*.

Many souls who left their homelands in advanced civilizations to assist Earth's less evolved souls have retained their fifth, sixth or seventh density spiritual and intellectual status. It is a sad note for all light beings throughout the universe that some of those advanced souls are the ones who devolved severely by reneging on their agreement to join the light forces.

Nevertheless, light is flowing abundantly on Earth, aided by the goddess, or feminine, energy that has been pouring in. This peaceful, nurturing, creative and gently unifying energy is mingling with the long-dominant forceful masculine energy that seeks success in all ventures by whatever means is necessary. Both energies have valuable strengths, and they are blending into the balance wherein all is light.

This energy blending has been exposing the vastness of greed, corruption and deception on the planet—those dark aspects in humankind that have perpetrated and perpetuated wars, disease, poverty, savagery, fear and ignorance for so long. When Earth exits third density around the end of your year 2012, she will leave that darkness behind.

Her destination is fifth density, where Gaia embodied as the planet you call Earth—she will be back home and contentedly orbit in the love-light vibrations of that high energy plane.

Gaia's Message

Last year when I was participating in a fall equinox global meditation and visualizing Earth radiant in golden-white light, I heard, *"Please record my words."* This is what I recorded:

I am Gaia, the soul of the planet you call Earth. Just as you, I can feel heavyhearted or lighthearted. For long ages I wept, when my spirit was broken. My people were hateful to each other and my body was soaked with their blood. I weep no longer because there is so much to feel joyful about, so much to feel thankful for.

My light is not yet in full force, my body is not yet balanced. That is because some of my children still are being hateful to one another. Some of them are without love, without compassion, without the understanding that differences can be absolutely splendid when harmony and respect flow along the heart-lines.

Yet, I am joyful because I am on a journey like no other soul in this universe ever has traveled. I am going home, and you who are holding the light that is helping me move steadily and quickly forward are coming with me. Can you imagine a greater distinction than this journey we are sharing? Can you imagine a greater excitement than our ascension? I cannot!

I asked to speak this day to tell you of my gratitude for all of you. You were chosen from a great number of souls, triple the number that could incarnate and participate. This level of light service never before has been undertaken. We are playing a part in the grandest show ever performed in this universe. I feel the humility that mingles with sublime satisfaction for a job well done—in the continuum, our job *is* completed.

As our travels continue, many wonders are in store for you and this world of ours. You have been told of many, so you can think of them and look forward to them, but actually living in the glorious times soon coming is beyond your imagining.

All beings in this universe are watching this unfold, did you know? I cannot imagine such a vast audience! All the souls of light are cheering for us, so we shall continue giving them a good show, an experience worthy of even God's applause. I share my heart with you and my love for you is overflowing.

Acquaintance with

Other Worlds

Extraterrestrial Assistance

What happens on Earth affects the whole universe, so it is of utmost significance to advanced civilizations that the dark energies that have held sway on your planet for eons become reconciled within the light.

In keeping with universal laws, assistance from one civilization to another can be given only when it is requested. Your heartfelt desire for a peaceful, harmonious world is your request—what is in your hearts rings out to the universe as clearly as your voices—and God authorized many nearby and far distant civilizations to come to your aid.

Your bewilderment about how to heal your planet's pervasive environmental damage also is part of their assistance mission. But *you are in charge*—Earth is your homeland and you *chose* to be there specifically to participate in this world transformation and spiritual renewal that is underway!

However, assistance from extraterrestrials started long, long before their infusion of the light that saved Earth's life more than seven decades ago. Throughout the planet's history our universal family has served in one kind of supportive role or another.

Members of some highly advanced civilizations had a hand in designing and establishing the flora and fauna, and human life on the planet derived from several civilizations' seeding programs. Among today's populace are descendents of those ancient residents, some of whom were gods and goddesses who chose to lower their body density by incarnating rather than remain as pure love-light essence like the rulers of the universes did.

During the eons when Earth was known as Gaia or Terra or Shan, twice negativity amassed in such amount from humankind's ungodly ways that Earth had to rid herself of that unendurable burden through catastrophic upheavals. In the first occurrence, individuals who had retained their light were rescued by their ancestors and all others perished.

The second time negativity became intolerable, the upheaval came in two separate incidents—the destruction of the once glorious civilizations on Atlantis and Lemuria. Some souls who lived during those eras chose to reincarnate before the planet's surface was once again hospitable, and they established beautiful living areas in Inner Earth. Others from those two civilizations have embodied during the last half-century or so specifically to help prevent another such catastrophic event.

The Akashic records, which contain every soul's lifeprint of each physical and spirit lifetime wherever in this universe it is experienced, are maintained and safeguarded by some of Ashtar's forces.

For long ages some of Hatonn's Pleiadian crews have been on rotation maintenance tours to insure the integrity of the light grid around Nirvana—Nirvana is the proper name of the spirit world you call heaven—that bars entry by rogue entities.

For equally long times crews from numerous civilizations have been monitoring the heavens for meteors and other small celestial bodies or debris that are headed toward Earth. When anything is of a size that could cause extensive damage, the crews change its course. After your air travel started, the crews deflected the trajectory of debris or dematerialized it if it posed potential danger to planes in flight. They also have rescued persons thought lost in ships at sea or planes that disappeared; the rescued parties physically entered a different "timeline," which is why they weren't seen again on Earth.

Extraterrestrial assistance came with unique swiftness and intensity over 70 years ago, with the massive infusion of light that kept the planet from spinning out of orbit into certain death. Because the in-pouring of light was available to all of Earth's residents, those who responded started generating their own light with greater forcefulness.

Along with beaming light to the planet until it is well within fourth density, various civilizations are using their technologies in a number of ways in accordance with Earth's more recent desires. For instance, when the Illuminati cause a geophysical event, the crews lay down an electromagnetic grid that distributes earthquake or volcanic activity and lessens destruction and death toll without reducing the amount of negativity released. In the case of manmade weather, the crews decrease the wind velocity of violent storms and steer them away from heavily populated areas along coastlines.

Remember the viruses called SARS, avian flu, swine flu and H1N1 that abruptly appeared on the scene with simultaneous media hoopla that each disease, in turn, was "feared to become a pandemic"? No pandemic happened because members of our universal family neutralized those laboratory-designed viruses and doomed the Illuminati's twofold intent—genuine pandemics with great loss of life and global chaos and fear.

Crews in your skies, who are there by the thousands and thousands, are using their technologies to reduce as much as possible the radiation from Japan's damaged nuclear reactors, and they rendered less harmful to marine life the oil that kept gushing into the Gulf of Mexico. They are ameliorating the toxic effects of weaponry and other pollutants, and a civilization appearing as cloud formations is leading the way in cleansing Earth's atmosphere.

As important as all those kinds of assistance are, perhaps the most vital help is preventing the Illuminati from using nuclear warheads to mount disastrous terrorist attacks. A dozen or so attempts have been thwarted by rendering the warheads impotent, sometimes in combination with missile malfunctions. This is not a violation of Creator's law of free will—it is honoring Earth's free will choice that there will be no more terrorism on the scale of "9/11."

Some of the strongest, most experienced light beings in this universe are right there with you. The purpose of their presence derives from their superior intelligence that gives them entry into fields where they can beneficially influence decisions and activities during this crucial time of Earth's transition. Some are working behind the scenes to guide the essential changes so that as many of Earth's residents who choose to accompany her into the higher planes can do so. Others are risking their lives by exposing various parts of the Illuminati's global network to free you from that insidious control.

Very few in your civilization know that several thousand people from other worlds are living on the planet. Since they look like any other person, the populace as a whole is in for quite a surprise when these visitors identify themselves in their customary appearances. Although they recognize each other from the distinctive auras that reflect their souls' evolutionary station, only the most energy-sensitive Earth humans can detect that difference.

Since the most distant sources of assistance have names you wouldn't recognize—some are musical tones mingled with pastel colors—I'll mention only the star systems relatively nearby where Earth's benefactors are from: Pleiades, Sirius, Arcturus, Orion, Lyra and Andromeda.

Now you can see how universally beloved and significant Earth is and how beloved and important YOU are! Still, what your benevolent brothers and sisters are doing is not a rarity in the universe—souls evolve through service to lesser developed civilizations that request help. As you continue growing spiritually and intellectually, you too will want and be able to help enlighten and uplift lesser evolved souls. That is only one joyful aspect of the magnificent adventures awaiting you!

Some of Earth's Benefactors

Representatives of numerous civilizations transmitted formal presentations for *Revelations for a New Era, Illuminations for a New Era* and *Voices of the Universe,* and all contain ancient knowledge and wisdom. Unquestionably that is important for us to know, and in accordance with God's instructions, some is intermingled with information about their respective civilizations and how they are helping us.

Often as the presenters were speaking, questions arose in my mind. Because they know my thoughts when we are connected telepathically—this connection is true of all of us and whoever we are thinking about—they answered, then proceeded with their presentations as if there had been no interruption.

Other times, at logical breaks, I typed my questions. Like my mental questioning, usually those pertained to the speaker's homeland location, environment, family life, cultural interests, recreation, employment, homes, animals, form of governing, and education. What they said about those aspects of their worlds is fascinating, but there's space in this "*short* but vital book" for only a little of that.

However their natural appearance may differ from ours, these members of our universal family speak of themselves the same way we do about ourselves—*people*. In Matthew's words:

When civilizations are highly evolved spiritually, their forms can only be beautiful. They may not look like the human forms you're familiar with and call beautiful, but they are indeed exceedingly lovely, perfect creations in their own sense of beauty and in God's eyes as well.

Prothero

This is what Matthew told me about Prothero: *"He is an ancient soul who has a high degree of knowledge in harnessing energy for electrical use. His love for Earth is inherent in his core essence connection with the planet from its beginning, and his expertise in co-creating far exceeds most others who also were involved in those earliest stages. None of his lifetimes on the planet were in English-speaking nations and most of them were long before that language even existed, so he quickly studied English because he wished to speak personally with you rather than use the universal translation mode."*

Previously Matthew had explained to me what co-creating is: Everything in the cosmos is energy fluctuating at one frequency or another, and that energy comes from Creator/Creation. *Co-creation* is our use of Its energy to turn our ideas into whatever form or condition is the focus of our thoughts (the universal law of attraction).

Prothero was the first presenter Matthew introduced who wasn't in Nirvana. He didn't speak at all about his civilization or send me his image, and I didn't think to ask him to do that. So I assumed that only in my imagination was he a very tall, thin humanoid without a tinge of color or glow in his white skin.

When I asked Matthew about that later, he said that what I had imagined was very close to Prothero's appearance. His people, who come from diverse origins and range from fourth to seventh density in soul evolvement, assist newly-forming worlds through their co-creational knowledge and skills.

The following are excerpts from Prothero's 1994 presentation.

Opportunities for accelerated experiencing in mortal body now exist that never before have been presented on Earth. Your feelings and thoughts, not only your actions, are more crucial than ever before in these waning years prior to the closing of this millennium.

....

Prior to this period in your planet's history, souls could spend hundreds or even many more lifetimes learning their chosen lessons, but now, time by your calendars is waning for mortal experiencing on Earth.

....

Here are guidelines for your preparation in awareness and wisdom to survive coming changes:

Do not be frightened! Fear is the opposite of love. You may think hatred is the opposite of love, but hatred is a byproduct of fear. There is nothing to fear! A vital transition of planet Earth is in process, and fear is detrimental to your understanding and to your thinking positive, enlightening thoughts. Following your positive thoughts with positive actions is of utmost importance for fulfilling the mission you chose for your lifetime at hand.

When you chose your mission, you had all awareness of the times ahead and you eagerly arrived on Earth. However, after birth you forgot your chosen mission lessons except at soul level. Within your soul full knowledge of the lessons is clear and awaiting your conscious attunement.

....

Do not shirk responsibilities intuitively known. These responsibilities are to family, to friends, to strangers and to yourself in accomplishing the plans your soul has in mind to follow. If you will meditate even for a short time to clear your mind of superfluous and disruptive thoughts, you will receive confidence in your proceedings. Your conscious connection is with God directly when you so listen and heed. *Allow the love of the Christed light to permeate your being.* This is yours for only the asking. ASK! Open your thoughts as simply as "God, be with me," and God *is!*

Menta

Menta worked with me in 2009 to condense her lengthy 1994 presentation, when we had four long discussions, without sacrificing anything she felt is vital for us to know. She said that during the 15 years between her original messages that are in *Revelations for a New Era* and the book's revision, her people have joyously observed the powerful effects of the light that they and other civilizations continuously have been sending to Earth.

Good morning, Ms. Suzy! I am here in the brotherhood of all humankind. We are your friends! The important message I bring to you is in alignment with the energies being beamed across the universe to heal your planet. Without this help, Earth would not recover from the insufficient oxygen in her atmosphere or the negative vibrations and chemical pollutants that are the result of the collective thoughts, actions and sensations of her humankind.

Behind this oxygen deprivation that causes a veil over your consciousness, negativity and pollution is the heavy influence of the dark forces at work most diligently and incessantly. There are within those forces true sparks of Creator, the Supreme Being over all the universes in the cosmos, as everything in existence comes from Creator's energy except darkness itself.

Darkness could not come from Creator, whose essence is pure love-light. Everything throughout the cosmos in form or without form, or as you say, "discarnate," starts with an idea, and the highest, purest beings came from Creator's idea to express Itself into those very first souls you call archangels.

In the Beginning all of the angels' ideas were in line with Creator's and together they made the lower angels and gods and goddesses. All of those souls were made of the same love-light energy as Creator. But eventually some angels had ideas to make horrible, miserable creatures and found much enjoyment in doing so. *Never was such a thing Creator's intention!*

But even when those angels made still worse creatures and lost their angel status by moving so far away from the light of Source, Creator kept Its promise about their free will. They and their foul ideas, which are indestructible substances called thought forms, became the gigantic energy field known as "the dark forces."

Yet always the soul sparks within those forces have been connected to Creator because Its energy is their very life force. Each universe is a microcosm of the cosmos, so ever since darkness began those untold eons past, all souls throughout all universes have had the free will to use Creator's infinite energy for either light or dark, according to their ideas.

Creator picked some of the gods and goddesses to be the rulers of the universes and co-create everything in them, and in this way you are inseparably connected with Creator through the reigning god of this universe. The only law Creator gave to those rulers is that always they must honor Its free will gift to all souls in their particular domain.

Therefore, you have the right to choose what to co-create with this god that you call by God and other names. Ms. Suzy, with respect to your customary name for this highest power in this universe, I will say God.

Using God's energy, each of you choose and create your life situations by your own ideas, your thoughts that are of light essence or of the dark, and in that same way all of you together make everything that is in your world. Some ideas produce sickness, pollution, wars and greediness, and the revelation will come forth as to what this kind of co-creation means for all humankind and for dear Earth herself. You have become mired too deeply in third density to hear and see and think beyond this low level sensing. That is a pity, because only a breath away there is a wondrous universe for you to explore, but the glories awaiting your discovery cannot exist within a *perception* that is narrow and confined in its vision and sensing. However, the higher energies now swirling around your planet offer a great opportunity to change that narrowness in outlook.

.....

Earth's cry for help was a weary sound of resignation, like a faint echo of a once healthy life that had become too feeble to call out loudly. That weak sound signified that Earth was near death due to her environmental conditions, and we wanted to help her survive and be restored to health. God authorizes a genuinely unselfish response to such a request for help, but no intervention is permitted except by invitation to participate jointly in the venture.

.....

We are more powerful than many others who also are helping to their full intensity, but their wavelength is less than ours, so we volunteered for a twofold mission. We are beaming in our own energy and also sustaining the light from those other sources once it is within Earth's atmosphere. This is essential so that your bodies can absorb the rays at cellular level and adjust to the higher frequencies Earth will be entering. This gives you the opportunity to physically survive during her ascension process that some call "the shift" and others call "the cleansing."

.....

We are a vast and powerful energy field of a billion or so collective souls. When we embody, we live on a planet called Retorno in a galaxy beyond the constellation Lyra. Our homeland is one of many inhabited worlds not yet seen by your telescopes. I shall explain why I say "I" and "we" interchangeably. It is because I speak with you as a soul self, but never am I separate from our group mind. No soul is considered better than another as all aspects of our mind are necessary for our world's stability and our ever-growing awareness.

.....

As collective selves we resemble a tree much more than a human because our "head" area is an abundance of sensors that look like flowers in a tight cluster. That is the "housing unit" of the group mind. White is the predominant color of this head area, but pastel colors also are seen—they are the colors of specialty areas such as the arts, technology, engineering, child rearing and so forth.

We are an array of the colors most closely identified with the primary talents and abilities and interests at a particular time, so the colors change to reflect the frequency in which we are operating. That is, it's the facet of the prism refracted into the color identified with that frequency.

Connected to the "housing unit" cluster and extending throughout galaxies are a billion or more fine "threads." Those are our soul-selves roaming the heavens in search of new knowledge, or more accurately, *remembering*, because at highest soul awareness level everything is known. All soul-self discoveries instantaneously and automatically are transmitted to the group mind.

When Menta sent me an image of her people, I told her they appeared to be a gigantic network of twinkling lights moving about like shooting stars.

You are seeing a good likeness, but within the minute scope of the mind's eye it is impossible to detect our vastness. Although we can move freely throughout the heavens forever twinkling, your telescopes will never see us because we are flickering lights rather than sustained light.

I asked if they can embody as individual souls and if any of them are on Earth in human form.

We could do that and look no different from you, but we have no reason to do so at this time because our assistance to you does not require us to be on the planet like the many "extraterrestrials" who are living among you. I don't wish to offend, Ms. Suzy, but we see as huge beautiful lights those highly evolved souls who left their homelands to "walk in" by agreement or who were born into human bodies specifically to serve Earth's needs in this critical time, and the few you do see are regarded as merely entertainment spectacles.

....

My people—different from you in appearance but of corresponding grace within—give you our assurance that our assistance will continue in peacefulness throughout the period of reformation in your world. Now, in fellowship and brotherhood, I leave our message within these pages for your contemplation and acceptance in the same loving spirit that we continue to serve Earth in her restoration to health and beauty.

Suzy, we are friends from so far back that you have no idea, but someday you will. All of Earth's peoples then will know their rightful place in our universal family.

Lazarus

Matthew spoke of Lazarus (Laz'-a-rus) as "*a soul representing the Lazarus energy, which is highly respected universally. This massive force was assigned by God to reduce the destructive effects of the negativity that has so polluted Earth that it almost killed her planetary body.*" The following excerpts are from a few of Lazarus' many transmissions in 1994.

We are not the only ones eager to help you and your Mother Earth continue on her ascension journey. Others in flagships and mother ships have been present in your atmosphere for well over half a century of your years. While some of these beings are merely curious about the drama unfolding in this solar system, most are friends who have come to your rescue. Like we, they come only with love and peaceful intent to assist you and Earth!

....

We are a group of souls as huge as your galaxy and with corresponding powers, yet we are speaking in terms we understand and you understand. It is the same truth brought by messengers from God in previous centuries, the truth of your godself.

....

We are in spirit brothers, we and you, and therefore

natural collaborators in God's service. We are among the millions of your universal family whose crafts have been surrounding your planet on "active duty" for fifty years or more, relieving Earth of the negativity that nearly killed her planetary body.

We combine our energy with other entities who also want to preserve Earth's life. We came en masse to breathe our energy into her lungs, which are the air, the atmosphere, to withdraw many of the pollutants that were killing her.

....

We are not warriors, we are more engineering minds. Our energy has been helping to stabilize the planet and hold steady its orbit through areas where other heavenly bodies could seriously affect orbiting stability. We harness, or level out, the effects of what you call "natural disasters" to prevent the widespread destruction that otherwise would occur.

We withdraw force from the energy fomenting beneath the surface that would produce volcanic eruptions of such magnitude they would blow up entire mountains and destroy surrounding towns. We stabilize fault lines so earthquakes are less severe—they still release energy, but do not destroy the vast areas they could without our softening interference.

We quiet the seas and temper the wind forces so you don't have the extent of hurricanes, cyclones and tornadoes and flooded coastal areas that you would if we did not do this. We alter the course of celestial fragments within impact distance of Earth. We keep a rhythm going that is required of all your life forces.

....

To describe the appearance of our group entity, energetically that is, imagine the effects of a high wind through tall evergreens, a strong sweeping motion at the top and a strong whirring sound, and along the ground, gentler movement and sounds. That is a good way to imagine us. There is no face, no form, no color, only sound and motion in our energy that covers an area larger than your solar system.

We wanted to evolve as collective souls but were limited by the low intellectual capacity of some members. "Group entity" or "group mind" means that all members may share the energy generated by the finest, but diluted by the weakest. Rather than exclude the intellectually weaker souls within our group, we elected to merge our individual consciousness into a major force with unity of purpose and direction. We have not regretted this decision and have learned that we can individuate, live as individual souls, and still retain the group soul focus toward the light.

Our incarnation began in Sirius—many habitable planets in that constellation are comparable to Earth in all essential life-sustaining ways—and we became a very small percentage of the Sirian civilization. Our group energy that wished to experience in embodied form did so by contact of physical bodies for conception and birthing.

Our whole energy never was nor is now incarnate, but the streamers that do embody resemble your white races in form and features, and in tenacity and mind power we resemble your red races. While physical stature is important because it determines activities of physical strength and interest, it is *soul identification* that is the absolute, and here we bow to our kindred spirits, your indigenous peoples.

Also we have lent energy particles to some souls who wished to experience in other civilizations or as animals. Many whales on Earth in past eras had our energy, but because of the slaughter that began some two hundred years or more back in your history, all of that has returned to our group energy and continues to serve Earth within our "greatest" self.

....

Our home in part is the one in Sirius, but over time we learned that Earth offered a new beginning free of intellectual pollution, a status not yet achieved in your linear time but already manifested in the continuum, so we are living among you *in spirit only*. Do not ever fear that our presence is as captor to you as our captive! NEVER! *We were led here directly by God to work in energy only.*

The ways you can identify with are in nature, physics, the power of combined natural elements. We are making our course toward the light more direct, without the deviations of war and conflict of issues, which is why God directed us to Earth. If only you people could see from our vantage point the energy you are wasting in your bickering and wars, you would instantly stop!

....

In this moment I am with you in energy only, but during these times of such enormous changes in the universe, usually I am in one form or another, depending on my service and location. For some time I have been aboard the mother ship hovering nearby Earth, but when situations are quiet, in a fleeting second I can be at home with my dear family in Sirius.

Nine years later Lazarus gave me a message for *Voices of the Universe,* and this is part of it:

All along we've been reducing as much as possible the toxins in chemtrails, radioactivity in weaponry and other harmful pollutants. Oh yes, we also had a hand in saving the Gulf of Mexico from dying after the oil rig explosion.

And we're always on the lookout for meteors and other small celestial bodies and debris heading toward you—I think you'd be amazed at the number we've directed away from you. We aren't alone in this work. Almost all of us who are nearby have been in on this kind of protection that began eons ago, when Earth started descending into third density's vulnerable zone.

I'll tell you about a relatively recent incident, a year or so before the turn of the century in your time. My troops weren't in on that particular save, but except for your civilization, it's known throughout the universe. An especially large speedy meteor was being directed at you by the peak of the dark forces—they had wearied of their slow-moving conquest of the planet and decided to just annihilate it. When your space brothers saw that this meteor had been pulled out of its normal orbit and redirected at Earth, they put out an immediate call to Menta's forces, who had the power to pulverize the meteor into tiny fragments that burned up before entering your atmosphere.

In several conversations, Lazarus and I had talked about his family, and I asked about them.

Suzy, you dear soul! My family is wonderful! Thank you for asking. I devoutly hope that when the first ETs make their presence known on Earth that people will be able to think of us like that—with families like yours, whom we love just as dearly as you love yours.

Icarus

Lazarus interrupted his transmissions to introduce Icarus, who could spare only a short time from his crucial mission elsewhere in the universe. These are excerpts from Icarus' presentation in 1994.

Good day, Mistress Suzy.

We were notified late about the cleansing and preservation project and arrived from our homeland Redondole (Ray-don'-do-lay), near Sirius, later than many others who also came to help Earth-Gaia-Terra-Shan.

It is our pleasure and pride to be involved. This project is of foreign nature to us as we have been confined for all time to other constellations, where growth is in goodness and truth. God has allowed us this privilege to assist in lessening the trauma of planetary changes and uplifting the consciousness of your civilization. We are eager to place our troops at your disposal!

....

Icarus, like many other names in your mythology, descended from fact. The mythological Icarus is so named because of his golden wings of wax, a symbolic inspiration that came from our space fleet. We are in possession of a fine fleet due to far-advanced intelligence and superior technology that derive from our fuller brain usage than your current civilization. This is not spoken egotistically, Mistress Suzy, only factually. Our power for fuel, heat, lighting—*all* needs—comes directly from sources provided by God.

....

We are sending you our image. As you see, we are not humanoid in appearance, but only in our natural habitat do we appear tall, rangy, silver and very, very thin, with large eyes and long nimble fingers. We do not much care for the "spider" of your thought, but it is your comparison and so we accept it.

We can embody to look exactly like any form we imagine or wish to imitate, including just like you. That is how many of us are among you already and you are not the least bit aware of it!

We are assisting in the cleansing by being in influential positions so we can make a difference in decisions that affect the environment, the pollution and industries, and in other ways that can reduce the negativity on Earth and therefore reduce the destruction of terra firma and seas.

We are part of a force in Earth human disguise that cannot openly declare its presence or purpose, which is the very salvation of your planet! We would like to be known as who we are naturally and no longer hide among you. However, it is not yet time according to our messages directly from God, who rules all major decisions in this universe and has His own timetable for optimum benefits to all concerned.

We are eager in all respects to assist and not take over any aspect of your self-governing that is according to the laws of God and the universe. We will honor all self-rule and decisions unless these are aimed—as so many are—at self-destruction and planetary destruction. Then we are empowered to technologically oppose those forces, to prevent what would be so traumatically destructive to the planet and lives.

....

Acting on Creator's mandate, the highest cosmic councils declared that there would be no more nuclear or atomic explosions in space, which have damaged souls even at such a distance from the explosion that you cannot imagine it. I speak not of temporal bodies, but of *souls*, which are eternal parts of God. Therefore, that one exception was made to honoring free will, and we would be part of the energy force that would prevent such a destructive attempt.

....

I asked Icarus if he would return to talk about his civilization's home, history and future among us.

We are more than happy to be here at God's invitation to contribute to your book and would be most happy to return at any time you invite us. We are on an invitational basis, as are all beings of light, so as not to invade the privacy guaranteed by universal laws. If you extend the invitation, we will return and discuss the information you mentioned and perhaps more of our own that you may not think to ask.

Now, with grace and love we take our leave. One day we shall greet you warmly in the streets of your cities and perhaps much sooner in your dream state. Good day and goodbye for the moment.

I didn't invite Icarus to return—organizing, indexing and editing the many transmissions became so ponderous that I forgot about his gracious offer. However, when I was reviewing the manuscript prior to the book's publication and came to his message, he told me that his people are encouraged about Earth's ascension progress—unfortunately, neither of us had time then to speak at length.

Many years later, during the book's revision process in 2009, Icarus greeted me again. He was in high spirits and said the members of his civilization living among us are fulfilling their assistance assignments and eagerly looking forward to the joyous day when they can introduce themselves. We didn't change anything in his original presentation, but once again there was no time for a long talk.

Prometheus

Matthew spoke of Prometheus as *"from still another origin far beyond Earth. His powerful and benevolent civilization has been given authority by God for the safekeeping of Earth's orbiting path, just as others you already have heard from."*

Long, long ago many visitors from outer space, as you call our worlds, came to your planet to investigate the environment for sustaining life of certain species. In time, Earth became well known as the paradise it was in those long ago times, and it became a placement of wonder, beauty and desirability in the hearts of many space explorers.

You do not know of these beings yet, some of whom are not what you would think of as human, but they are nonetheless intelligent beings of great advancement in many ways beyond your conscious minds' ability to imagine. These souls are seeking their spiritual paths and are further along in their self-discovery than you in your own searching in this respect. They never will harm any soul seeking the same path and, like many other powerful sources, bring only greetings and a pledge to assist you and your planet home.

We are among these lighted beings and are the forefathers of some of your own human selves. We are from a planetary system in a constellation named Orion. There is no individual aspect of our civilization, but there is perfect harmony in the rhythmic motion of our searching ever toward the light. We have evolved into the needlessness of physical bodies, and our advancements in intelligence and spiritual truth-knowing has enabled us to materialize in thin strata formations that represent the cumulative soul essence and minds of billions of souls.

....

We understand that it is difficult for you to think of intelligent beings as odd cloud formations, yet we are in this appearance of proximity to Earth to exert the force required for maximum assistance.

The clouds will be your stratus-cirrus variety with "puffs" where an energy vortex is required to lessen the intensity of pollution from the chemicals and other toxins in your soil, water and atmosphere.

....

We will be working along with but not in unity with other powers from far beyond your planet. We will remain as long as the stabilizing forces provided by us and others are necessary to keep Earth orbiting regularly and your polar areas from tilting so drastically and far afield of current placement that an instant ice age would befall Earth.

....

Welcome the newcomers in strange forms and from strange places. Know that among them we are foremost in sustaining the faith of your forward movement on the lighted pathway. We do not sanction fear and, in fact, we cannot approach an aura of fear as that energy is anathema to our core nature of peacefulness. We pledge our assistance in God's service and thus your own when our presence is evident above your horizon.

....

Welcome not only us, but all the other souls who also have declared their support for your physical and planetary safety. This is all I can persuade you to do, and it is my only purpose in addressing you this day. In the Christed light, promise and faith, I am most truly your servant in love, Prometheus of Orion.

During Prometheus' and my review of his 1994 presentation, we agreed it should be included intact in the 2009 revision of *Revelations for a New Era.* He also spoke about his people's current activities, and we added that to the updated edition.

Oh yes, we are in full force as the need is great for our energy to reduce or neutralize to the greatest extent possible the quantity of toxins abounding everywhere around you. It is impossible for you to breathe pure air or for your marine life to live in pure waters, and even the organically grown produce cannot escape the proliferation of pollutants. But with our assistance and others' as well, the prevalent pollution is not nearly as damaging as it would be otherwise.

The cleansing is not yet in final stages, but the headway is close to miraculous from the first moments when Earth cried out for assistance. We are privileged and honored to be in the forefront of this cleansing effort insofar as our nearness to you.

We maneuver around the skies in search of toxic trails to dissolve so the particles that fall to Earth's surface carry less damaging elements. We still are reducing the pollutants in the seas as well, but this effort is more discouraging because of the sonic currents that are so harmful to life there. And we impart our energy to other forces on the ground to give them invisibility as protection in times of danger.

So you see, we are very much in your midst! And joyfully so, as the years between our first talk and now have produced such great enlightenment and uplifted spirits among the populace! All of us in your "space" community of families look forward with great anticipation to introducing ourselves in a form that you will see at first with amazement and then embrace as the brothers and sisters we all are. The lighted pathway is leading to grand excitement as the Golden Age of Earth is nearing!

Agnes

Throughout Agnes' presentation, I felt her energy as lilting and tender—so very different from the "powerhouses" who previously had transmitted messages for *Revelations for a New Era*. Although she didn't mention that she was sending me her image, I saw her as a petite young woman with delicate features and a gentle smile, and a light blue scarf covered her head and shoulders—reminiscent of paintings of Madonna and child.

I greet you in peacefulness and attentiveness to the needs of Earth consciousness in all its radiance of her Beginnings as paradise.

....

My civilization was partly responsible for the populating of Earth in its earliest seedings. We always have held most dear not only the humans living within this atmosphere, but that paradise of a homeland selected for your breeding and experiencing.

It was intended that someday we would reunite with you in all glory and recognition, but there has been no attempt on your part to encourage such a reunion. This is from fear and loss of memory, and it does not change our relationship, it does not lessen our love and brotherhood. So that tells you most clearly why we are here at this time of severe changes.

....

We will assist in ways individual rather than collective. Our purpose is to reunite with those souls who came from our own beginnings. All souls here are precious in God's regard, so we do not denigrate one soul and uplift another arbitrarily.

It is as if a family on Earth called in the cousins and aunts and uncles so all are under the grandparents' roof for reunion. It is a natural selection, is it not, and you do not feel it is necessary to invite all who may pass by the roadway beyond? So it is with our mission and purpose. Yes, of God, in all ways and always.

We will approach not in our form, as the welcoming parties are rarely happy to see a stranger in the kitchen. First, we are already with you. Second, some of you have seen us in radiance, recognized in an energy that is warm and embracing.

The recognition is not as a brother to a brother, but as a sense of wonderment and smoothness of the experience. Deeply, yes, this is indeed brother to brother, but at the surface level where you are thinking most of the time there is only wonderment at the sensations that are coming with greater recognition and frequency.

And what do we accomplish by this means? Reunion pathway. Hand in hand on a deep level we are walking with you toward the light. This is toward junctions you will recognize at soul level, a sense of familiarity without explanation, and later with conscious memory that will be welcomed, however startling. It will be the *"Aha!"* from your soul.

....

Yes, you are lost. And when we tap into your hearts and minds to give you a tiny spark of light to follow, often you do not wish to make that deviation from the path you have carved for yourselves. This is a disappointment for us, but it is not our place to do more than be the spark. We cannot drag or push you into seeking the spark.

....

But now is a critical time of reassessing your pathway. It is a lamp that we bring to you to light your way back to the Oneness. In God we find selves, always! But first we must recognize that God is within each soul. There is not a massive being of strong opinions and strict rules, as your churches often portray. The God within is our connection in family, our connection in soul and love and the lighted way to unity.

We are here to be your guides, if you so wish. Yes, we have chosen those among you whom we will guide, if desired, if permitted, because you are our family and many others are not. There are among our family many millions, however, and there are other progenitors such as ourselves whose families also will be contacted in the same way as we are now reaching our own.

....

God's assigned missions to us are to reach all souls who will greet us. We may never be seen in a dense form, or we may, but do not doubt that we are present in all strength and willingness to walk hand in hand with you until your basic memory has returned and you will welcome the companion along the journey to the LIGHT.

When I started reading Agnes's message during the revision process, I felt the same lilting, gentle sensation I had 14 years previously. Agnes welcomed me and said it is extremely gratifying to her people that many of their Earth family are responding to the love energy surrounding them. *"All the heavens await your self-recognition as multidimensional souls."*

Aeschyles

During our chat prior to Aeschyles starting his presentation, he told me that our pronunciation of that name is the most similar sound to his name in his language.

Now is the moment when each soul on Earth must choose whether to live within the light or the darkness. Among you are souls whose light is so radiant that we can detect in simply our viewing that the soul is in a high station. We see twinkling lights, the announcement of souls awakening to their godselves. But we see also many souls whose light is only a dim spark because they are still slumbering in the delusion of separation.

This era at hand is being heralded by us and all other light beings as your opportunity to triumph over the darkness that so long has been clouding vision and hearts. The unveiling that even now is well underway is due to the light of God and Creator shining ever more and more powerfully upon Earth. My people stand with you in your journey to rise with your planet into the higher levels of light. That is the message I have come to bring to your people, dear Suzanne.

....

Just as you, we inhabit only one planet, so you know that definitely we are not of those majestic, almost unimaginable powers with whom you have talked before, those whose powers range across galaxies and are universal in effects. We have no power to do other than what we do, which is to travel and impart our experiencing and survival to others in similar states of war in which once we also were engaged. There is great wisdom to be gained from our history, which is so similar to your own.

Because the history of Aeschyles' civilization parallels what has been transpiring on Earth for many millennia, the Council of Nirvana asked him to tell us about it. His verbatim account during our several conversations in 2000 and 2003 is too lengthy to include and excerpts out of context would be meaningless, so here it is in my "capsule" form.

Seven million years ago in our linear time his people's ancestors established a small colony of spiritually advanced souls on planet Catalon (Cat'-a-lon), which he said *"in your term of 'light years' is not all that far away."* During the millions of years that the population increased, greed and power mongering entered their nature and gradually the civilization descended into *"competition and conflict, then to violence, brutality and wanton killing"* until it reached the brink of self-annihilation about 50,000 years ago.

"Our planet had only a few souls who had not reached that self-destructive depravity and loss of spirituality, and it is thanks to those few souls who held the faith that we are the culture, the harmonious, peaceful and God-aligned civilization of today.

"Those few savior souls were born into *our populace, not born of it, and in this way, they could be likened to those souls who are most revered on Earth for their godliness and savior essence. From that same level of Christed energy from which Jesus, the Buddha, Tao, Mohammed and others who came to Earth with messages from God, so came those human saviors to us. They were able to slowly bring us back from that most*

precarious near-self-destruction level and open our eyes to our inseparable connection with the universe."

The difference between the history of Aeschyles' civilization and ours is what makes Earth's ascension unique in this universe. With extensive, intensive, continuous assistance from many other worlds, we will be accomplishing in about 80 years what took his ancestors almost 50,000 years to do without that kind of help.

We are one small planet among, oh, "mega-zillions" of places wherein life abounds. Some is like ours, some is like yours, some is higher than we can even imagine, some is so primitive that it could hardly be called life, and some is at such a base level in morality and spiritual awareness that you may not wish to even know of it.

We are fourth density, but we are very nearly graduated into fifth, and therefore are seeking an impetus to rise into that higher elevation of awareness and clarity. We have been told by the greater council that this can be achieved by such as I am doing in this moment, on behalf of all my people, willingly offering our assistance through relating our experience that, if heeded, can be of immeasurable value to you.

....

In mass, or density, we are much the same as you, but we are more uniform in form and features than you. You are varied in these respects because Earth was populated by several diverse extraterrestrial civilizations. Only one such civilization started the population program on our planet.

Aeschyles sent images of two women. Both were stunning in

formfitting white gowns and had a self-assured pose and demeanor. They were tall, very slender, had skin like porcelain, vivid blue eyes, perfect delicate features and bright red lips. The only difference in their appearance was that one had a mass of long, dark curly hair and the other had glistening blonde hair that flowed well below her shoulders.

The women of our culture sent those images of themselves via my thought waves for transference to you. But you do see them as they are, and quite clearly. They may choose how they wish to appear by virtue of our having successfully developed our abilities to manifest through visioning, or visualization. Our women are not, in your fleeting thought of them, "ladies of the night" in temperament or attitude or activity, be assured. I believe they meant to convey purity and still a passionate essence to you, as that is their true nature.

Our women do not usually wear the apparel you saw. That would be for formal occasions, and just as you choose less formal clothing for other kinds of activities, so do our women dress more casually and conveniently for theirs. Short, loose colorful robes is their usual preference in their homes, and they wear longer, more fitted outfits when work or interests take them into what you could consider social or business areas.

Aeschyles sent me an image of himself—he is as stately and handsome as the women are poised and beautiful. He addressed my thoughts:

You are questioning the attire in my image, which you perceive correctly as the short armor of ancient Roman or Greek warrior days. I chose this because it is appropriate for what I shall speak about, the warrior temperament of Earth peoples. That temperament is as outmoded in the universe as this outfit I am wearing. I could wear a business suit representative of money, job, career—business endeavors leading to financial wealth, which is your idea of success and the fulcrum of your efforts and desires—and that, too, would be outmoded in this day of global and universal change.

Then he sent another image.

I appear now in raiment to represent the seekers of the light of the universe. They do so that they may be consciously elevated into that glorious state of Oneness and share that light by radiating its energy into all reaches of the universe. So you see me in flowing and shimmering raiment, with large wings of feathers, all in white with golden glow.

The wings are not representative of angelic status— angels themselves do not have wings, as you have been told. The image of wings is symbolic of soaring beyond beliefs and philosophies not based in truth, but rather based in perceived separation. Leaving those limitations is to soar in the radiance of love and soul connection, the essence of the spiritual Oneness our civilization has achieved.

....

I was more than willing, I was *eager* to make this considerable space journey to be with you and spend this while in exchange of information. It is not a great undertaking—that is, the mechanics of the trip are not—and most surely I am joyful about being invited to participate in this God-mandated flow of information through these books.

....

I made this journey alone on a small craft that is so similar to those you see in your entertainment forms that you might not be surprised to see it in your airports. That is, you could recognize it from "Star Trek," for example. With the assistance of higher civilizations during these past 50,000 years of our rising up from near-self-destruction, we have mastered the mechanics of astrophysics—engineering; fuel, which is almost entirely solar; and time/space energy direction. Our commonalty with you is the materials we use, which you have on Earth but have not yet combined in the correct alloy proportions to achieve what we have. We can see forms of advanced technology in existence there, but they are hidden by your governments.

In your time/space consideration, my starting point would be four light years from you. However, both your "time" and "distance" in miles and light years are your designs alone and do not apply beyond your planet. So, travel to Earth and Nirvana within the continuum, where your time and distance calculations have no basis, requires only a day and a night of your calendar for a leisurely trip.

There is the mathematical aspect and then the engineering aspect, and all is within the capacity of manifesting, the materializing and dematerializing for rapid movement and then rematerializing once in the atmosphere of destination. Our spacecraft and travel are just as common to us as your modes of transportation are to you, but ours are more efficient, more comfortable and more accessible to all of us than vehicles and travel are to your people.

First I went to Nirvana, where I dematerialized the craft, and my travel between there and Earth has been astral. It may interest you to know that I have seen thousands of other small and even some immense spacecraft in the area of Earth, some so close at times that they hover only feet above your surface without your awareness.

Always the relationship between animals and humans, or other classifications of cognitive beings, is of essential value in spiritually evolving souls in all civilizations at levels up to seventh. At that level and above, the souls have no form. That is, there are no dense bodies, but even so, the animal and human or suprahuman energy is closely aligned. Plant life also, as that cannot be ignored in the overall essence of either God or Creator.

Each living soul—each *life* is more accurate—is composed of energy, and since energy is of Creator, every creation is also of Creator, and in this universe, of God. Thus, a tiny ball of fluff is just as much a creature or creation of Creator, or God, as any other. Its charm and open, loving nature and loyalty—the same characteristics you admire in a person—are recognized and respected in our animals, and our interaction with all of them is on a plane much higher than your own.

Yes, there are animals for food for the humans of our world. But the treatment of those animals throughout their lives and most surely, the means by which their lives are ended to become human nourishment, are with

caring, mercy and painlessness, and with our thankfulness for the nourishment that they willingly provide.
Sadly, this cannot be said for the treatment of most of
your animals.

Earth animals, too, are sentient beings far beyond
the awareness of most on your planet. The non-recognition
of this truth allows many there to see animals as "dumb
beasts," neither needing nor worthy of love, kindness,
loyalty or mercy. This lamentable situation that has
caused much of the trauma of Earth herself will change
as your civilization rises into the awareness of the interconnectedness of *all* life.

Do not forget the order of plants in Creation, because
that interrelationship gives and receives in equal measure.
Your Devic kingdom, unseen and unknown to most of
you at this point, is closely allied with the caretaking of
your plant kingdom. Few there have recognized the
sacredness of your trees and the other plants, which
have their own consciousness and thus know of their
value within the entire planetary life system.

....

Our civilization recognizes that the zenith of balanced
selves is androgyny, which requires the assimilation of
both male and female energies, including sexual. Thus all
attractions of mates are recognized with honor, and on
Earth there is great opposition, even danger presented
to couples of the same gender.

Last year when Aeschyles and I reviewed his original material
—and made no changes—he gave me an enthusiastic update on
his people.

In unison my people rose into the spiritual clarity of fifth density only recently, and what an inspiring and awesome occasion it was, the ceremony of thankfulness for what we have experienced, everything we have learned thus far.

We rejoiced in the simplicity of advancement that is in such stark contrast to the truly mammoth, arduous journey the population undertook many millennia past as they struggled to leave the darkness of third density and finally made it to fourth, where nothing of dark nature can exist due to the light intensity. Progressing to fifth density is a matter only of gaining greater awareness of the Beginnings through self-discovery—actually, remembering what we know at soul level—coupled with assistance to less evolved civilizations.

The changes I mentioned are additional means whereby we can assist other populations, not only by relating our history such as with your people, but in technological ways that came by virtue of our unified self-discovery process. All knowledge is in the universal mind, and by agreement of all of us, now our scientists and engineers are absorbing knowledge in new avenues. Since we haven't focused on technologies heretofore, this expansion of our knowledge in these respects is exciting, and sharing it with others will be most meaningful.

....

When the absorption is completed to the satisfaction of our people, we will be able to manifest more swiftly and grandly whatever we envision. Actually, the *visioning more grandly* is the advancement, and that is how our assistance to others comes into it. We will have more to offer those civilizations that are just beginning to develop technologies. We will be born into those civilizations but consciously retain our spiritual clarity, intelligence capacity and expertise that will elevate our persons to positions of leadership in technological areas. However, our service will be twofold, and the more important aspect will be steering developments in alignment with spiritual growth.

Saminten

Matthew told me about his visit in Saminten's world prior to my meeting Saminten, so I already knew a little about his civilization. When he told me its name is Hyanita (Hi-a-ni'-ta) and its "home space" is Costrayna (Co-strain'-a), he added: *"That is an embarrassingly feeble facsimile of the sound of those names, which are lilting music with slight gradations of beautiful soft tones. Mother, this is like describing color to a person who was blind at birth, I want you to know!"*

Saminten asked me to call him Sam—he's delightfully personable—and during our several talks in 2002 and 2003, some of which are in *Illuminations for a New Era*, he was in Nirvana. In relating his reason for being there, he also gives us a peek into Earth's spirit world.

I am not a transitioning soul from Earth, but my residence for the time being is Nirvana. I am here in collective energy form, but not as a mass of amorphous souls rather sliding around. Yes, I am an embodied "fog person" of whom Matthew has spoken and I am visiting here as an emissary from my people.

We are indeed a civilization, but I believe you would not think of us as "people." Matthew described us well as a mist or vapor, dense above the ground and increasingly less dense as it rises into wisps, always moving in a rosy golden glow and with charming fragrances that meander as we do ourselves.

The vapors, shall we say, gather into shapes so there is some form to us, but no weight or clear demarcations.

The cloud formations, let us call them, are gleaming silver with undertones of pale crystalline blue, like a fine diamond refracting countless tiny sparkles. Not everything about us sparkles or our world would be too brilliant to behold, but the larger configurations do have an exquisite luminescence.

Farthest into our atmosphere, where the strength of the mist is least, is our haven that is equivalent to your Nirvana. You may remember that Matthew said that we have no DNA programming for aging or death and our sanctuary realm is for rejuvenation only. We go voluntarily for restoration of strength to better perform our service of beaming light into the universe for civilizations in need of it. After ages of this beaming, the strength of our souls diminishes and the formations gradually become only wisps that naturally rise into our highest atmosphere.

This area is of a more gentle glowing essence, somewhat like a florescent pastel painting in slow and gentle continuous gliding motion. Never is the light dulled, but it is dimmed, if you can see my difference. Always there is the glowing essence of the souls as they waft in delicate fragrances and the subtle colors, as even our palest tones always are of iridescent nature. This reflects our soul evolution, and our auras are just as intense as our "body" essence.

....

Hundreds of millennia past my people were not in this "vapor" or "fog" essence, and the spiritual aspect of ourselves was miniscule compared to today's grand volume of God-connection awareness. Our connection is no greater, please understand, but our *awareness* of it is. That is a most important difference, and it is a similarity that we share with you in this time of your growth of spirit.

We merely existed then. We had no purpose for growing and frankly, we had no interest in helping either ourselves or any others. It was a time of recovery for us, but we were unaware of that as the reason for it was not in our memory. Our minds had been somewhat destroyed, and the memory aspects of our mental abilities had been taken, actually lifted right off our DNA by thieves of the highest dark order in the universe.

Interfering with the growth of a soul is the only infraction that constitutes what you call "sin," and altering the DNA of a soul is the ultimate interference with its growth. It has such major damaging repercussions for the affected souls and it incurs such heavy karmic pressures for expiation for the causing souls that nothing in the universe compares with it.

We languished for eons while our strength of knowledge and spiritual sparks were rejuvenated through the efforts of volunteer physicians of the universe's highest light capabilities. They rejoiced as they saw the beginning of our memory returning, and our signs of intelligence and stimulation coming through the "fog."

It is not by chance that you have expressions like "seeing the light" and "being in a fog," as these are manifestations of a depth of understanding—remembrance, actually—that you do not associate at all with your idiomatic expressions. But in many instances these go back to eras way before your civilization of today, even before life of any beautiful nature came in the first seeding program of Earth.

....

It is rare that part of our selves embodies for any purpose, but to visit here in Nirvana at the invitation of Matthew and the Council is a glorious opportunity to see this beauty so we can add to the natural beauty of our own sanctuary realm.

With our level of intelligence and technology development, we could embody in a twinkling, but that would be such a backward step for us that we would not be interested. However, for me to come here and fully experience the many glories of Nirvana, it seems appropriate and very gratifying to have this body that I manifested in keeping with the beauty and radiance of the others who are here.

It allows me to touch and feel, to drink liquids and to feel the many animals brush by me with friendship and to touch the flowers that are incredibly sweet in their aromas.

....

We live in a galaxy "near" your own. This is a return to the distance scheme you have devised that doesn't exist beyond Earth, so "near" and "far" are not suitable ways to give you our location relative to yours. However, we are not as close to you in *energy* as many other civilizations are.

....

We have no ground as we are not on a celestial body, but rather in a protected space. It automatically is protected because of our high energy registration that no entity of darkness could approach.

When Sam and I spoke again, several months later, he had returned home.

With rare exceptions my people have not had the experience of embodying because their souls never were in lower densities. And none have shared life with a multitude of various civilizations such as I met in Nirvana, but through the essence of our collective selves, they, too, share the sensations I had in body.

There is no division in our awareness of each other and our collective knowledge and experiencing, so even while I was in Nirvana, my people were sharing my visit.

....

In antiquity, even before universes and their god or goddess rulers came into being, Creator gave forth Its gift of free will with the intent that it always would be the province of each soul. However, when the darkest of the dark forces emerged, it used its own free will to claim the collective free will of souls who became curious about the dark and then became entrapped by it.

This subverted Creator's intent. After eons of light constantly being beamed at those darkest souls so that of their own free will they would release their captives, Creator acted. A few years ago in your counting, It withdrew the collective captured free will from the topmost stations of darkness and restored it to the individual souls.

Thus the original intent of Creator's gift once again prevails, but Creator also decreed that there will be one exception to honoring all free will choices. This unique exception will curtail any souls' choices that would damage innumerable other souls by means of nuclear detonations anywhere in the universe. Not damage to bodies, understand, but to the *souls* themselves.

In many times prior to your recorded history, some civilizations were intensely destructive to many places in the universe. Worlds were destroyed and widespread damage was done to souls' DNA, the ingredient that you understand as imparting distinct individuality to each soul. Creator has decreed that never again will that happen, therefore Earth will not be destroyed nor any more souls damaged by that means.

However, the health of your planet had become precarious otherwise. God, the ruler of this universe, which is one within the cosmos over which Creator rules supreme, is authorizing all civilizations who so choose to answer the cry of Earth for preservation and restoration. Without help, your precious planet would perish from the predominance of negativity that was strangling her breath and dismembering her body.

Thus many of us fairly close by, even though usually from galaxies "light years" distant in your term, have heeded this call. Many diverse areas of assistance are being given by civilizations whose advanced spirituality and technology are helping to rid your planet of the negativity as well as help her stabilize and recover from its effects.

These waning days before total release from negativity are the most exciting and uplifting for Earth since her beginning, when gods and goddesses reduced their high energy registrations to adapt to living in human form in your planet's environment. Retaining their original multidimensional capacity would not permit the fully human experiencing they wished, and so the souls "downloaded" into heavier density. Over time their desired spectrum of flourishing and reproducing in totally incarnate forms became possible.

Sometimes benevolently and sometimes not, those god and goddess souls reigned over the seeding programs of a variety of civilizations and the introduction and evolution of the human root stock. As conflict grew and former spiritual awareness diminished, the density of the planet's atmosphere was lowered by the resultant negativity.

Twice all life was lost and the planet revived to start anew. A third time was not God's intent, and Earth's own soul, Gaia, did not want that, and now we have reached that point whereof I spoke, when she cried out for help and many of us willingly answered.

....

And now I shall tell you the part my civilization has been playing as a collective group of souls in Earth's revival to her former health and glory. We are strengthening the resolve of each life in the kingdoms of animal or plant or mineral that wishes to rise into the higher density with remembrance, clarity and evolutionary soul status. Cellular changes have been in process for several decades, and assimilation of what is happening with the fuller light now beaming can be greatly assisted by the leveling process or leavening agent we can provide.

....

The light on Earth has been accelerating in sustained amount for the past year of your timing. It was necessary for this sustained situation to occur so that more souls could awaken to their godselves and rise along with your planet into fourth density. My people have been assisting joyfully in this process.

The importance of this ascension cannot be overstated. The souls who rise with Earth will be living in the paradise that once flourished there so gloriously. The souls who do not reach the level of light required for this journey with Earth will be removed to placements for remedial lessons in consonance with their lower energy registration.

It is lamentable that your science sees little connection between the power of the spirit and their developments. There is no separation of spirituality and science. There cannot be! The ingredient of souls is light from Creator Source, and light is the scientific expression of the love that is the parent, or "manufacturer," you may say, of light. Your science recognizes only the directional use of light without understanding its true property or origin. So this division in belief needs additional resolving, and my people have been strengthening the assimilation process.

What is occurring there is an amazing sight from here or anywhere else in the universe! The new sparks continuously evident are the souls lighting up with the connections between their souls and their minds. You will appreciate this spectacular necessity as you rise into the lighter density, but for this moment, let me say that it is fireworks of the most magnificence in power and the same in the rejoicing of all light beings.

....

I asked Sam if he could describe his civilization in numbers of souls.

Not nearly as easily as you can, with a body for each. However, in our collective essence we could be considered as having about 100 million souls, although that seems rather few. It has been so long since we considered ourselves as individuals that no doubt that figure is a poor estimate, much too low. You see, each wafting "part" may be the essence of one or a million souls as there is no mental or emotional division.

....

Our population doesn't increase by any reproductive methods you might be familiar with, but we welcome any and all wandering souls or free spirits who find us and would like to enter into our essence. Since we are not limited by space, the newcomers never are crowding in. Because there is limitless freedom at this height of evolution, any soul who wishes to leave for additional growth may do so, and in our collective awareness that there is no separation, those souls enrich us with their self-discoveries anywhere in the universe.

....

Sam, do you consider any souls young or old?

Suzy, you heard me laughing and I'm delighted to see you joining with me in amusement. I am aware that you speak of "old souls" there, but nothing could be further from an accurate description of *any* soul than anything ascribed to "age." What *is* different is the learning, or remembering, status of each soul. Every one of us started with Creator's first sharing of Itself insofar as the elements for all creations, which are love and light. So we, like all other souls, are as old as those elements, which literally are age-*less*. The souls who join us totally meld into our essence and bring no age into it.

....

Without compromising the inviolate essence of each of us, we truly are One in love, thought, philosophy, desire, aspiration, discovery, inspiration, pathway back to God and Creator.

....

I must smile at your question of whether we might be sharing a single thought because it is more like sharing the whole universe of thoughts. And yes, indeed we do communicate, but any sound would be tones, not speech. In keeping with the gentleness of our movement, the tones are like your most charming lullabies, but barely audible. Telepathy is such a natural way for us to communicate that when toning is used, it holds the awe and joy for us that hearing symphonic music does for you.

Then how did you learn such articulate English, Sam?

And so we laugh together again, Suzy! I knew your question before you typed it and felt your embarrassment as well as amusement as soon as you did yourself. Yes, at our height of awareness we know all languages of the universe, including those without speech, such as ours.

....

You decry the loss of time that seems to be zipping by and another loss you lament is memory. Neither of these aspects of third dimensional awareness is being lost, dear ones. "Time" never has been as you devised it with 24 hours each day and 12 months in a year and so forth. This has served you well, but no longer is this happening. Your time structure is collapsing as energy is moving at its lighter density speed, and your periods of light and dark are coming with more velocity. So rather than time being lost, it is speeding up.

The memories that many of you speak of as "gone," are not. With the acceleration of everything within the universe, it is natural that the cells of your body are reacting to being lifted into a higher survival mode. Most of all, this is affecting your brains—the computers that turn on your thinking and reasoning processes—and this is necessary! The light being absorbed by your cells is allowing your brains to slough the layers of forgetfulness and programming that have denied them full functioning ability.

If you are not experiencing any memory loss or a sense of scattered thinking, then you are stuck in the third density that not much longer will be the status of Earth's being. So it is desirable for you to feel not quite firmly in touch with the reality of the day or the environment.

All of Nature, which is everything with a soul, is evolving. Earth's soul—her own inviolate soul and the collective of all souls living on the planet—is evolving. Only if you speak with animals and trees and hear their response can you appreciate that you and they—every life form that is receptive to the light—are moving into the lighter essence of all existence.

....

There are no divisions of past, now, and what is coming. It is more accurate to think in terms of learning and knowing what next needs to be learned. And even this is not altogether correct, as peeling away the layers of forgetfulness is not a learning process, but a *remembering* and *allowing* process.

Last year, just as I finished reading Sam's lengthy chapter, he spoke:

Beloved Suzy, yes, we meet again! Your thought of me connected us immediately, and it has been a privilege for me to share your enjoyment as you read again our earlier conversations. You know that for me, scarcely a "blip" has passed in the same timeframe that to you is almost nine years since we last spoke.

....

The service we have been extending to your people all along has continued, and it is with humility that I say that our light, which has greater intensity and directional ability than many other civilizations' beaming capacity, has been instrumental in convincing some persons in influential positions to accept the light. I know that

Matthew has told you about them, and he is correct that not in all cases did they embrace the light enthusiastically, but they no longer are serving the darkness.

It is our honor to assist our brothers and sisters, those who finally accepted the light and all who are benefitting by that reduction in the lingering darkness on the planet and within its residents.

Hatonn

Hatonn, who has been a friend ever since my telepathic connection opened in 1994, is a handsome 10-foot tall intergalactic fleet commander from the Pleiades. He's also in charge of communication between Earth and the rest of the universe.

In chatting prior to his formal presentation for *Voices of the Universe,* he told me: *"Especially now, with everything speeding up, everyone needs to know that their spiritual connection with God isn't achieved through mental exercises or incantations or invoking the help of ascended masters—it simply **IS!** Every soul is a part of God, every one **IS** connected with Him! How could it be otherwise when it's the physics of the universe at work here?"*

I am telling you the simplicity of the answer to your soul-searching: You are a part of God and your connection with Him is your birthright. God IS. You ARE. You and God are ONE. How much more simple can it be? Your soul knows this, and you need only to align your conscious self with your soul, your godself.

You may search through books to learn how to make the communication connection, but those are merely others' ideas of how to reach a stage of spiritual awareness, and that is not necessary. It is as simple as your ASKING! Say, for instance, *"God, I am you, you are me, so please let me hear you."* Or say nothing, just feel it in your heart—God hears that just as clearly. Allow your mind to be still and listen to your soul giving you God's message.

....

As for searching for God's "will" in your life, as so many of you do, you could say that since you are God in fullness and He is you as a part of Himself, yes, He has a pathway for you. But your own soul as the God part you are *chose* the pathway it needs for growth, and the purpose of your life is to consciously discover that pathway. Conscience is your guide, and so is your intuition.

After Hatonn finished his short message, our conversation continued into other topics that became a different chapter in the book. The following are excerpts from that chapter.

How are you coming along with you multiple responsibilities as communications director and intergalactic fleet commander?

Communication is the more challenging by far because of all the wrong ideas folks have about telepathic communication, the DISinformation coming through, and that mountain of layers I was talking about. The commander function is easy by comparison! We're all in a holding pattern, performing our various technologies that are helping your planet recover from the eons of neglect and abuse and ignorance.

Hatonn, is the information about the ascended masters being taught accurately?

Suzy, most of them are APPALLED at much that is being taught about them! If anyone knows how faulty the idea is that they must be called upon to guide and instruct on the pathway to God, it is *they themselves!* At Matthew's evolved state, he ranks with the "ascended masters" but he doesn't consider himself this and for good reason—the souls who are given those exalted designations *don't* ascribe them to themselves!

I am *not* saying that the knowledge and wisdom in the *authentic* messages from them is not important! It IS! I'm saying that it's not necessary to go *through* them to reach God!

Are any souls here now really reincarnations of any of the archangels?

The Christed light that is within every soul born into a physical lifetime is a new, inviolate, independent essence. The Christed light may be an *aspect* of one of those higher souls, to be sure, but to say that any person is the total incarnation of *any other soul* is totally incorrect.

What about the various soul growth stages? I've heard there are twelve—I think it's twelve—parts of the soul and each has to evolve in a set order.

Oh, *my!* A soul is a soul is a soul! It *never* is "in parts"—it is its complete own entity in fullness at every stage of growth. What is not understood is that the power of each soul enables it to be in all lighted space simultaneously, and the less a soul has evolved, the less of that ability it has.

Serapis Bey

Primarily known for his lifetime in Egypt as an architect pharaoh, Serapis Bey is with us *"etherically,"* as he told me before beginning his presentation for *And Then God Said...Then I Said...Then He Said....* For wider dissemination of his message, God asked me to include it in the 2011 revision of *Voices of the Universe* and in this book too.

You may associate my name with ancient architecture, and rightly so, yet a builder of much more importance to you than of pyramids and such, ah yes! Most notably in your history as a designer and builder by talent and trade, I shy away from returning in a body for more construction.

Instead I am lending my energy, or perhaps "infusing" my energy is more apt, to receptive ones who may or may not realize that their motivation and inspiration are in part in cooperation with me. It does not matter if they do not know. All that matters is that they beautifully express their talents in inspired ways.

....

But return I do in this manner to whet your appetite to the self-realization and self-actualization of your individual building, *your soul evolution,* by way of LOVE in all undertakings to restore Earth to her former health and beauty.

....

As architects who step-by-step design and build your destiny on this unique stage of your eternal life, do so with the assurance that I, Serapis Bey, and heavenly hosts without number are with you, adding our light to yours. Keep smiling—ah, the radiance of love in a smile!

Janos

Before introducing Janos, Matthew told me that he is from an eighth density civilization in spirituality and intelligence. They also are highly advanced technologically, and some of their scientists have been "filtering" their knowledge to our scientists who are receptive. Like us, Janos' people came from diverse civilizations.

I believe that your homeland can benefit by knowing the history of my own. My people are named by our planet and it is one and the same name, Galatia (Gal-a-ti'-a). We have ascended from lower fourth density and I know your world is currently ascending from third into fourth. That is why my information is intended to be valuable for your knowing and consideration as to how you can use my people's experience to benefit your own.

So many years ago in your counting that I cannot tell you exactly, my ancestors were a warrior people. They were not always of that nature, nor were they of lower fourth density spiritual and intellectual attainment. To start at the beginning, people of several civilizations who landed on our planet were attracted to its beauty and peacefulness and many settled there. At that stage of Galatia's evolution, it was similar to Earth, with large landmasses and many seas, and the planet herself was of fifth density.

Harmony was the basis of life for a while, but eventually some members of one civilization wished to have power over all the others. The majority, who were being increasingly constrained, obviously did not want that arrangement to proceed. Discussions were not fruitful and thus the war scene came into being. As it continued, and *because* it continued, Galatia could not prevent her planetary descent in vibrations as it was in accordance with the energy being generated by her life forms.

At that time my people could live for many thousands of your years. Their bodies did not die because their DNA had no patterning for physical disintegration. Rather, they designed their bodies to best suit their selected missions, and when those were completed, they retired those bodies and manifested new ones in keeping with their new chosen missions. When they had accomplished all missions possible for their soul growth on the planet, they moved into lighter space for higher experiencing.

However, in the lower density to which they had fallen due to the tyranny, the development of lethal weaponry and then the onset of war, bodies were killed before the souls had completed their missions. This was such an abrupt departure from formerly that the population was severely traumatized. Billions of young bodies were being annihilated and the souls were in confusion, seeking other worlds suitable for continuance of their unfinished missions.

The pure in heart petitioned the intergalactic high court for relief, and this is the response:

As the free will of those who would plunder and destroy cannot be denied, those of you who oppose their rule must act upon your divine godness to generate enough light to dissuade them from continuing. Failing that measure, you may call upon God's higher beings to assist you with their light intensity and it will be given.

The pure in heart did not prefer to give higher beings the responsibility to assist and they declined to call upon God's stronger forces. Later they regretted that so greatly that as one voice, they cried out for assistance. It was given with that first request, but by that time the population was reduced by over one-half and the once-beautiful planet was in ruins.

The abundance of light beamed to Galatia was more than the warring minds could bear. The battles stopped, but the warrior proclivity that remained in some souls caused their bodies to die, and the souls went to placements for remedial learning. The survivors were strengthened in spirit by the in-pouring of light that also was restoring health to their damaged planet.

With the horror of millennia of combat as a stark reminder of life on a planet starved for light, the people wanted Galatia to rise into dimensions where light was steady in its intensity. They learned that their desperate cry for help was answered because, by universal law, the power of their collective desire could not be denied. They actually had *created* the help they cried out for.

They learned that each soul is responsible to chart its own way through self-discovery and self-determination, and the more souls who desired to live in the light, the more quickly that would be accomplished for the civilization. There were stragglers, to be sure, but the unison of thoughts in the majority slowly and surely lifted Galatia from lower fourth density to her station in eighth.

Your situation is much like that of the ancient civilization from which I descended, and like our planet, Earth as a planet is a living being composed of all souls who live upon her. Yet our planets are souls themselves as well, and if they wish to be free of their civilizations' free will destruction by exercising their own free will, they may choose to rise above it to the station where their souls came into being.

It is my knowledge that like Galatia eons ago, Earth has chosen to be free of the energetic baggage that would end her life if it continued. The laws of the universe permit planets to ascend out of their suffering that is caused by the life forms upon them, and those life forms must individually make their choices to ascend or descend. There is no middle ground. You have received messages that Earth is leaving that low density of spiritual awareness that permits warring and destruction to occur. It is now up to you individual souls there to act upon your own saving.

Janos told me that his people are individuals, not a collective soul civilization, and of the five trillion, about half live as free spirits anywhere in the lighted universe. Although his people who live on the planet don't need bodies, some choose to have them, and he sent me an image that is representative of most. There is no distinction between male and female: a tall, slender icy blue luminous body that looks like an upright ant with long slender arms and fingers and no legs.

The long slender arms with long slender fingers have functions well beyond yours. They are for accessing and putting into storage the universal knowledge that we have rediscovered up to this moment in our evolution. It is as if the entire body is a brain, to compare with your organ for storing memories of everything you have learned, and the arms are the conduits, or major entryways of additional learning that we retrieve from the universe. This would be like your most sophisticated computers that hold the many entries of information that you input. Some of our people, usually the elders, choose to have no arms. Their entire bodies can receive and simultaneously act upon information.

The stored knowledge is compacted within our bodies, like your knowledge is within your brains. The decisions about how to act upon our knowledge is inherent in our composition and could be compared to your minds—the thinking, reasoning part of you that works with the brain's stored information to decide the best course of action.

You saw correctly that we have no legs. They are not needed, as we move about only by the thought of where we would next like to be, and simply the image in the thought transports us to that destination.

Still another way in which our civilization differs greatly from yours is in our creating of children, which is through the focused thought forms of the "baby" soul and the parents. Only the parents and the soul to be "born" participate in the decisions about the new body. That is not to say that God is not involved, because each of them is a part of God.

The decision-making is similar to the soul agreements made by families on Earth insofar as attitudes and aptitudes, but of course, not the automatic genetic inheritance. Also like your agreements, the soul first is made aware of growth stages yet to be accomplished to attain a balance in its experiencing, and based upon that, the soul chooses individuals who will provide the most optimal nurturing and environment.

When that soul finds two souls who agree to be the

mother and father, all three focus intense energy upon a shared vision of the exact body the soul wants to inhabit. This is a co-creating process that starts with the "baby" soul's image that is projected to the parents. Although the image I sent of myself is a popular body form, any other style that equally serves the information gathering and storage purpose may be selected.

The creational materials are universal elements that, by the power of the thought forms, are formed into the design and function of the image in them. Making a body actually is a simple and rapid process, Suzy—it requires only the clear image and the desire and intent of the three souls to manifest it.

....

At this level there are no secrets, yet there is privacy. Just as you have public records, you also have personal matters that are not known if you so choose. All souls who wish to have a "new" life in the family send out their desire, which is a distinctive addition to their auras, and all souls wishing to incarnate can see which embodied souls may have interest in welcoming them. So can everyone else notice this interest, but it is respected as these souls' private matters. Usually the "baby" soul has discussions with a number of potential parents before making a choice.

....

The baby's thought forms are inseparable from its soul, so in that sense it could be said that it is "inhabiting" the body during the manifestation process, which itself is very rapid. What takes time is the collective concentration on the body design ideas so that all thought forms become exactly in attunement. A soul does not need a body for life itself, as that is inherent in the essence of every soul. It is only for experiencing physically what cannot be without some mass for functioning that souls choose to have a body of some sort.

Among your people, there is great misconception about "life" and the difference between a soul and a body. You have a process called "abortion" that some believe is the destruction of a new life, and there is argument about when a soul enters a body being formed in the womb.

No soul's life ever is destroyed by ending the formation of a developing body. Bodies grow independently of souls through the natural laws of physical mechanisms reproducing in accordance with the cellular programming of each civilization.

Souls are not restricted to incarnating in a specific civilization. A soul's spiritual evolutionary status automatically puts it within a certain vibratory level, and it chooses a civilization within that sphere that can provide the experiencing needed for its advancement. The greater the spiritual evolvement, the higher the light station within which a soul may choose the civilization for embodying, or living as a free spirit member.

Souls whose spiritual growth needs are within the third density of Earth or other placements of similar vibratory status, have a number of choices regarding bodies. They may reside around the parents even before conception takes place, and after conception, they may enter the fetus to experience that growth sensation.

If that kind of experience isn't needed, they may

remain "outside" for other kinds of experiencing prior to the birth, but with a soul contract "claim" on the developing body that other souls respect. If a soul enters a developing body and then reverses that decision, the woman experiences a miscarriage.

A soul may inhabit a developing body until imminent birth, then decide not to continue in that body and a stillbirth results. Also, a soul may make one of those decisions, experience what it requires emotionally, and in agreement with another soul, will exit and the second soul enters until miscarriage, stillbirth or live birth occurs. A soul with a "claim" on a developing body may permit another soul to reside in the body to experience the growth and birth sensation, then that soul leaves and the first one takes over the physical life.

These various situations always are by agreement with all souls involved, which of course includes the parents and any other family members, and the purpose is to permit chosen experiencing to several souls at the level they need. Abortion, like all the other stages from prior to conception through a viable birth, provides opportunities for the participating souls to experience the attendant emotions that fill voids in their experiences to that moment.

Bodies have a life force independent of a soul, and while it is an unusual situation that a body lives without a soul, this can happen. Souls have the choice to enter a cloned body or not, and if not, the clone still seems like anyone else because the brain and all senses and motor abilities are functioning.

Another example is when injured or ill people are comatose. The soul may choose to remain with the body or not, and if not, as long as nourishment is given, that body continues to live in a vegetative state until it dies from deterioration of cells.

....

Suzy, I have seen and also felt your astonished reactions to all that I was telling you about my people, especially about our "birth" method. Yet at one time the bodies of my ancestors were much like your own and reproduction methods and souls' choices were much the same as you have today.

To address your mind's question about the "time" for that evolution to happen, in your linear definitions, it could be considered billions of years. However, those definitions do not hold in the universe, where we actually are those ancient ancestors as well as being the souls we are in this moment. I cannot explain this in any way that you could comprehend that ALL is in this very moment.

....

What you and we have in common completely is free will and conscience. Those are the birthright of every soul throughout the universe. Without use, the conscience loses its functioning ability and the consequence is demonstrated in the abusive use of free will.

....

No aspect of ourselves dies and so we have no need for a sanctuary realm like Nirvana. What we do when we have experienced the degree of balance required to move beyond this life is move to another world in the same or higher density that will offer additional learning opportunities. Our bodies served us well and we transmute their energy into whatever other form will serve the people.

Janos, how many levels of density are above you?

I don't know. I am aware that different schools of thought on Earth have decided how many levels there are and their numbers differ, but it is very unlikely that any could know something that even at this station we do not. We can tap into the universal mind and comprehend only in the measure that is to be our next level of self-discovery. To skip around would leave voids and create misunderstandings of All That Is.

....

Our light intensity is forever available for sharing, Suzy. Not only is it not diminished by our sharing, it is intensified when it is received by any soul. It is not necessary to make this request to us by name. That is, your people do not need to know about Galatia or direct a request for help to us. All that is needed is for them to have in their hearts and minds the desire to live in love and harmony with others. That is the invitation to us and our light is instantly with those beings.

Light also is purposefully directed. Many, many civilizations, including ours, have the ability to direct light from any placement to those who are assisting Earth with their own technological developments.

....

The desire in any prayer goes out to the universe. The energy of that desire attaches itself to matching energy and brings that back to the person who prayed, although it may not be in a recognizable form. What many of you consider prayer is not the full extent of the universal law. Every thought and feeling originating within each soul creates thought forms that operate according to this universal law.

Although energy is completely neutral of itself, thought forms attach to its currents like tentacles and steer the currents toward like thought forms. The two matching types of thought forms unite and come back to the originator. When the thought forms are based in love, more love returns. Harsh, mean-spirited thoughts and feelings work the same way.

....

It makes no difference which name is called upon to give aid or is given thanks. Light is without boundaries. All prayers reach the Source of this universe. The light within our people, like that of all others in lighted space, is instantaneously touched by all who have opened their hearts to receive it.

Horiss

Horiss is a reptilian commander Matthew had met at a conference in Nirvana many years before he introduced him to me. The Council of Nirvana gave Horris permission to speak on behalf of the lighted members of his species.

It is known by some of your people that certain of my civilization are fearsome creatures that have been causing all manner of evil upon your world for endless time. We are not proud of that truth, and I have been requested to speak on behalf of our greater numbers who equally oppose the influence of those dark members. We, too, think of them as dark because of their actions, and we are in combat with them to rid their influence on your planet and all the rest of this part of the universe.

It is possible that of all who oppose their darkness, we are the most vehement because their actions reflect upon us as a total civilization. Those members are not in the majority and are not representative of the rest of us and it is not how we wish to be portrayed.

....

All souls in this universe derive from the same One Source, Creator, which makes all of us inseparable aspects of Creator and each other. God has told you that He is the amalgamation of all souls in this universe and loves all in equal amount. I say God to you, Madam, because that is your name for the ruler of this universe.

That equality of love is true from our experience, as we first petitioned to God to eliminate these most foul of our brothers from this universe. He has no authority to do this and likewise, no desire, because all subsequent soul aspects of those original ones are indeed elements of God.

The darkest souls of my civilization entered this universe from another in an energy blending of the two universes that was meant to be mutually advantageous by a sharing of light to advance spiritual clarity. Some souls resisted this opportunity and now in this universe, they have become God's responsibility to bring light into them. That makes it our responsibility to fight against their continuance in darkness.

....

What entered was the soul energy with dark thought forms attached. It is not only the reptilian civilization in this universe that this kind of soul energy entered, but it is primarily this one. They were attracted to it through the universal law of like attracts like, and the attraction on this end was our civilization's inclination to see strength in maintaining powerful defense forces of great military might. The souls with darkness that are influencing Earth humans are the reptilians that have made clear to other belligerent souls that Earth is solely their territory in this conquest.

....

We are well informed on events in many civilizations besides our own. Earth is of special interest to us, just as it is to many other civilizations of individuals and of collective souls, but it is by no means a self-serving interest. My people want the banishment of the dark influence on Earth to be replaced by peaceful means of living among all of Earth's inhabitants, and not to bring to you another source of troublemaking.

Our military might in numbers and technology could subdue yours in a day, as a description of our capability. However, ours is solely a defense force, and its purpose to defend rather than invade is the vital element of difference between our two worlds. This is further proof of our warm feelings, which extend to civilizations beyond our own.

....

When I say "my people," I do not mean that we are representative of all reptilian populations any more than Earth humans are representative of all human populations in the universe. I am speaking now only of the people residing in my world.

We reside on a planet in this galaxy that is as near my solar system's sun as Earth is near Sol. We use the energy of our sun much more efficiently than you use the energy of Sol. Instead of your various forms of power generation, all of ours derive from our sun. Yours also can, and as you progress in awareness of this, that will come about. Also, there is no pollution from any source anywhere on the planet, not on the land masses nor in the seas, due to our technology that prevents such contamination rather than makes an effort to clean it up.

Our home planet is called Lacone (La-cone'). It is as large as Uranus, to make a comparison that still is beyond your perception, but that tells you it is much larger than Earth, and it is about the same density of Earth in form and substance.

....

To describe us, we are of a height not dissimilar to your average height, but we are uniformly slender except our females who are bearing children. The skin tone is pale blue-gray, which is pleasing to us although it is unlikely that you would find it so. Our most distinctive features are our eyes, which are large and dark.

Male and female forms and features are much alike and with little variation in any. We do not have a mixture of races as you do and which creates the great variety in your appearances, but that is not the reason we are so similar in ours. Our collective choice is to look alike. Long ago we learned that differences in appearances can lead to prejudices and discriminations, and with our inclination to be a defensive people, we chose to eliminate elements over which we had control so that civil conflicts would not arise to weaken us.

....

Our children are conceived and born in the same manner as yours, but their intelligence at birth permits speaking soon afterwards and fine motor skills start to develop immediately. So at a very young age, about five years in your time calculation but with maturity commensurate with your adults, they no longer are dependent upon parents for protective attention and guidance. It is the love of family that bonds us and results in our children staying close to home long after they are self-sufficient.

....

While it is true that we are serious-minded and are not given to "frills," we are not without warm feelings. Our children are as precious to us as yours are to you, and our mates are the same. We are a monogamous people. Mates are judiciously selected and know each other very well before aligning as partners, thus separations rarely happen except by the death of one.

We enjoy levity and many forms of entertainment in which a whole family is participating, so you know that the sources of amusement are suitable for even the youngest minds. Music is important to my people, and none of it is blaring and discordant noise.

....

As a summary of the intentions of my people, it is this: We do not often speak of our convictions and our nature, we live by them. At heart we are warm, peaceful, respectful and helpful, and that is what we look forward to showing you one of these days, when you are ready to welcome "strangers."

When I reached Horiss' presentation during my revision process last year, he greeted me warmly and was much more at ease than in our first meeting. Here is most of our short conversation.

I am happy to be with you again, Suzy, if I may call

you that. It has been more than seven years since we last spoke, and as we reviewed my message I picked up your mental question. Shall I answer now?

Very well! Yes, we have made satisfying headway in "lighting up" the reptilians in your solar system. Of course not us alone, but in concert with all the light coming from far distant sources and all the light beings surrounding you and those among you. It is to our great liking that some of the dark ones of our race have left your planet and by choice are being rehabilitated in spiritual sanctuaries, including Nirvana.

We are diligently working to convince those remaining to give the light a chance and I cannot say that we are yet satisfied with the results of our efforts. Soon Earth will be in a vibratory plane where their bodies cannot survive, so you will be free of them by that means.

We applaud that, of course, but our greater interest is in persuading them to accept light. Like other spiritually evolving peoples, we shall not rest easily until every member of all reptilian civilizations in this universe has abandoned dark proclivity. It is in the interests of all civilizations that we continue this quest.

Are any dark reptilians still on the planet leaning toward the light? Not the most hardened ones, but those in lesser positions of power are wavering in that direction. No, I prefer not to identify any in either category, but you will see for yourselves as time passes.

And another question is in your mind, so I shall continue. It is possible, but unlikely, that I shall visit Earth any time soon. My interest in the quest I mentioned along with assisting in programs to uplift my people spiritually are foremost. However, when I feel a sufficient measure of success, my family and I may vacation on Earth when she has been restored to her original beauty. And I thank you for inviting me, Suzy.

Two Other Advanced Civilizations

For 14 years Matthew has been traveling astrally in his etheric body or as a free spirit—a soul who doesn't need an etheric body—or in a spacecraft to physical civilizations throughout this galaxy and others. The following are his descriptions of two other highly evolved civilizations that answered Earth's call for help by beaming their intense light to her.

Mother, I am greeting you from a magical world outside your galaxy. Ordinarily civilizations' invitations are for the purpose of my evaluating and assisting in upgrading their spirit realms, but this invitation was extended solely for me to visit, a respite from my service mission.

The magnificence of these souls, their spiritual clarity and environment is beyond the comprehension of even some other highly evolved civilizations. While they may know about the existence of these souls, they have not attained the growth that offers a frame of reference for relating to life in a world where all souls are completely attuned to the love essence of Creator and God. This is the kind of world I am visiting.

The souls here, whose individuation began in cosmic antiquity, eventually chose to be an indivisible collective mind and heart, so to speak, and function as an entity rather than a mass of individual souls who share the same intentions and goals. Their unification enables them to direct their energy as a powerful force field across vast distances to reach civilizations that most need this assistance.

In this sense, you could say that these souls' "leader" is the Supreme Being of this universe, for only at that ultimate and infinite plane can it be determined where the need for light is greatest and authorization given to direct it to the struggling civilizations most needful of healing love and enlightenment.

These souls could live in an evanescent state, but with their ability to manifest any type of body they wish that is compatible with their evolvement station, they chose a distinctive form. However, because their bodies vibrate at such a high frequency that third density vision cannot detect them, you would call this an amorphous, or discarnate, civilization. The body style they chose is a slender cylindrical "torso" that is more an indication of a shape than an actual shape because it shimmers in opalescent waves that comingle with the waves of all the other millions of cylinders.

The energetic "reach" of each—and you cannot conceive of it as it cannot be measured in your concept of distance—varies only to show the length of time each soul has been in the civilization and not the degree of spiritual and intellectual attainment, which is uniform throughout the collective souls. However, that degree of awareness keeps growing and expands the "reach," thus growth and change are inherent in life even at this height of evolution.

The cylinders are "storage silos" for light, and extending from the top half are golden filaments that connect with "blossom clusters" of sparkling iridescence. The clusters are memory banks that contain the combined experiencing, knowledge, talents and other abilities of the collective mind, an instantly accessible library of all light thought forms within the universal mind.

As you know, I manifest a body that fits into the civilization where my service has been requested or, like now, an invitation of the vacation sort. But I am here in my etheric body, which is attached as an "appendage," as it were, to one of the most ancient souls.

When they wish to communicate other than the customary telepathy, they "speak" in majestic musical tones of such softness and purity that nothing on Earth can compare. At this station and some beneath it in spiritual clarity, vibrations of consciousness are expressed as tones and pastel colors, and the atmosphere of joyousness, peacefulness and unity far exceeds the sensations that any dense body can feel.

These souls have no DNA patterning for aging, illness or death and there is no reproduction. The population grows through souls who are at the same spiritual level and are attracted to this force field by the universal law of "like attracts like," and all visitors who want to remain are welcomed. If souls wish to move onward for other experiencing, they are celebrated for their time in the civilization and bid a loving farewell with an open invitation to return at any time.

Their homeland, if it can be called such, is simply the space in which they meander throughout the universe. As they do so, their power wafts undiminished as they create the subtle beginnings of new worlds for souls with lesser awareness to evolve into in whatever physical forms they choose for the growth experience they select in pre-birth agreements.

My reason for describing as best I can these souls and their magical world, which it is to me, is more than a picture post card inscribed, "Wish you were here," although I do wish that for you as being here is inspirational beyond words; and it is more than enlightenment about a world for your wonderment.

From the moment Earth cried out for help and God instantly authorized many civilizations to respond, just that swiftly these souls started beaming their intense light to preserve the life of your planet and all her life forms. That they did so and have continued for almost seventy of your years shows their unconditional love for each soul on Earth and the importance of each of you to God.

———————————

Mother, I want to tell you about the beings I've met who have so captured my heart and my interest. These people are of the most gentle persuasion I have ever met! As you are seeing from the image I'm sending, this being could fit into illustrations in your comics or animated films, and I'd like you to type my description "for the record."

The body is like a tall cylinder—no curves like shoulders or breasts and no indentations like a waist—and there are no feet because these beings don't walk, they glide over surfaces like hydroplanes. They are not really glowing, as you're thinking, but there is a radiation that is not a regular light but rather an energy surrounding them. That is what propels them also. They are much less dense in form than you, but not as light as I am—if they were on Earth in their homeland bodies, you could catch glimpses of them in the right light.

The men and women don't have the variations in features or forms as do Earth and other human civilizations, but there is enough visible difference between the sexes so that I never confused one for the other. They speak with their mouths, just as we do, but they have no ears—they hear with their small antennas, which also help them control their direction when they travel in body—and the hair is smooth and tight to the perfectly round head.

You can see that their eyes are huge by your standards and so deeply gentle that they are almost without expression, but they didn't start out that way. They grew into this due to their evolved vision into what you call future and what they call growth. They can see for distances that you cannot even imagine, nor can I, because their vision extends throughout this universe into other universes.

They give live birth, which you might think is rather primitive for such an exalted spiritual and intellectual station that this means of reproduction is not necessary. However, their nature is such that they wish this intensity of bonding and closeness both as a union and as the birth process, and so by choice they reproduce biologically rather than by cloning or any other process for creating progeny.

The nurturing of their children is with such love that no child on Earth has ever known this constant gentleness, guidance and devotion. That height of emotions and sensitivity simply isn't possible in Earth's lower density.

Spiritually these people have attained a beauty that is pure joy to be near. The energy created by their loving nature is as radiant as ever I've seen in Nirvana at its most glorious. They do not live quiet lives as in dwelling only in thoughts and feelings, but they don't hustle and bustle about as you do. Their assistance to other civilizations is beaming love and light wherever they see a void and hear a cry for help to fill that void. This is what they have been doing for Earth in response to her cry for light so she wouldn't perish.

The following are Matthew's replies to my questions about that civilization.

They could be called suprahuman as a generic term, but that doesn't describe their spirituality aspect. A lot of suprahuman civilizations insofar as evolved intelligence and technology have no spirituality whatsoever, or such a minute amount that it's barely perceptible. Maybe *ultra*human would be a good term for these people, because they are a highly advanced human civilization.

....

They number about 40 million, perhaps a few million more—it's a very, very small population—and they live in a tiny planet that revolves around a number of suns. This is a strange part of their homeland planet, with the gravity situation so different from Earth's where there is interaction with only one sun. There is no gravitational in-fighting or tugging among the energy layers at that height of light, and all is in such harmony that these beings can almost be considered as taking a leisurely trip with little side jaunts and stopping now and then to smell the roses in their planet's revolutions.

....

The name of these exquisite beings and their world is the same, but I don't know how to give you this even phonetically because their language—communication is better—is in soft lilting musical tones and not word-sound syllables. Nevertheless, I'll try. Think of *la la tra la la* in beat, or rhythm, and a parallel sound of *do re me me re do* over and over. Those sounds in tandem resonate to something close in vibration to the name of these people and their world.

....

Their planet is about the farthest from you it can be and still be within this galaxy. But then again, Mother, you know that what you call distance doesn't exist "out there"—it's all a matter of energy alignment. Actually, it's realignment, alignment, realignment when I travel both within the Milky Way and to other galaxies.

....

The environment is absolutely breathtaking, simple beauty in keeping with these souls' purity, gentleness and vision. By "simple" I mean it is not cluttered or very uneven in elevation, nothing is harsh or jagged, such as mountain peaks or canyons, and everything is immaculate but definitely not with a "sterile" look. The bodies of water are shallow and crystalline pure and the different pastel shades of fine sand are visible.

The range of colors in everything from flowers to the sky is beyond description! The sky is ever-changing in tones ranging from the slightest tinge of pink or coral and gold to myriad shades of blue that sparkle like sunlight on rippling water. Your aurora borealis is not a good comparison by any means, but its changing colors is about as close as I can come to explaining the difference between that sky and those of Nirvana and Earth.

....

The animals here wouldn't be recognized as such on Earth as their forms are in keeping with the peoples' forms—sleek, radiant, and little variation in size or configuration. They have no fur at all and they also have disproportionately large eyes. Their soul energy, too, has evolved to the extent of "supra-vision," and their intelligence is astounding. There is total telepathic communication between them and the people. Actually, the animals' soul evolvement is such that they could embody as humans at a high station, but their choice is to experience as they are within this culture where they are respected in keeping with their spiritual attainment.

....

Yes, some of these people have embodied and made visitations to Earth only to bring light and higher level energy to you, but being there is not necessary for serving Earth in that same way. However, at their high energy station, embodying as a handsome human on your planet is as quick as a wink if that is what they choose to do.

....

There is no limit to their life span. At their spiritual level aging doesn't exist in the cellular structure because it no longer exists in the thought patterns. I think you would consider the purpose of their sanctuary haven more in the nature of a spiritual retreat or a solitary vacation in a setting of unsurpassed beauty, as leaving embodiment for them is voluntary and done on a respite, not a permanent, basis.

They may reincarnate in a different eighth density or more highly evolved civilization or they may remain as the population increases. The choice is each individual's and it is based upon the good of the entire population.

....

I have an open invitation to visit these people whenever I can, and because I am enthralled with their essence and their homeland, I would love to do that. Only the extent of my new responsibilities has prevented my returning to the joyousness of being in that height of sentience and service. But I shall indeed return when I can. Being among these souls in their surroundings would be the greatest inspiration I can imagine for everyone on Earth to "live the good life," spiritually speaking!

Former Residents of Earth

Since our definition of an extraterrestrial is someone who lives somewhere other than Earth, everyone who used to live here is now part of our extraterrestrial family. In *Voices of the Universe*, Cal, Grace and Jeremy—the names are fictitious—speak about life in Nirvana and how their respective services are helping Earth.

In those cases, like all others when family members asked me to speak with their loved ones in Nirvana, Matthew connected my energy streamers with those of the pertinent souls. Because he no longer is living there, I can't receive messages that require that kind of connection.

Ithaca, who was in Nirvana when Matthew introduced us in 1994, isn't helping us in the ways that Cal, Grace and Jeremy are. The Council of Nirvana requested that Ithaca speak about cosmic, universal and planetary history.

Cal

Cal arrived in Nirvana only a few days before we first spoke in 1998, and he was just settling in. So other than a personal message to his family about his easy transition and welcome reception, he had little to say that is relevant here except that he had signed up for a course in electronics. The following is part of our conversation last year.

I know you're updating the book, Suzy, and I wanted to add my two cents about how we're seeing your world from here. The changes since I came 13 years ago are phenomenal! All of us in these higher parts of the realm see how vastly the light has increased all over the planet, which is continuously advancing toward the entrance of fourth density.

There's not a definite line between third and fourth—it's the area where the last "energy wisps," I guess you could say, of third get defused in the first, stronger wisps of fourth. There's enough difference in the frequencies though so that no negatively-based entity or condition can slip into fourth. Of course you know the ascension doesn't end there—Earth will keep right on moving through fourth to her destination in fifth.

I also want to tell you something I'm doing that I think will interest you—I am one of the monitors of activities on the planet that Matthew has spoken about. My interest in electronics naturally led to my particular field, weapons. The thousands of us in this field who home in on missile sites and weapons stockpiles around the world are trained to know whether their vibrations indicate a state of "ready to go" or not.

Our individual notes are entered into a computer system that swiftly evaluates them and gives us a "read out" of our collective observations. When everything matches, we telepathically transmit a report to our colleagues on the planet, the ETs in civilian and military positions who have access to areas we report on. They add finite details and telepathically communicate all the information to the space crews surrounding the planet who use their technology to act on that information from their "ground crews."

This 24/7 operation—that's in your linear term, but ours is simply constantly—is how missiles with nuclear warheads have been destroyed or caused to malfunction every time since September 11, 2001 that a terrorist attempt has been made. Many times they've also prevented far less destructive weapons from functioning. These efforts are allowed because they're in accordance with Earth's choice that wars and hostilities wind down, and in honoring that, God authorizes these kinds of intervention.

Grace

A mutual acquaintance who shared Grace's interest in ETs and UFOs kept sending me questions to ask her. These excerpts are from some of our many conversations in 1999, shortly after she arrived in Nirvana, and the following year.

I am more eager than I could imagine while I was there to tell you about life *here!* No one there can do justice to the marvels of this place. It is awesome! I did believe that something lovely would be in my next life, but I couldn't begin to imagine HOW glorious it would be!

....

Suzy, Mark called you, I know that. I admire his interest in the discovery of alien life and I can tell him, *Keep trying, Mark!* There are troops like you wouldn't imagine and we can see the effects of their work to save Earth from collapsing due to all the roughhousing humans have been doing in their ignorance and belligerence and greed there.

....

Some of them are on the ground right there with you. They don't look any different from the majority of people, but they sure are different in their capabilities! In most cases, they simply agreed at soul level to substitute their higher light for the denser essence of Earth-born folks, and that's why such marvels keep appearing on the entertainment scene, for example. But there are others too, in all areas where influence is necessary for bringing about the changes for more peacefulness and kindness and truthfulness on Earth.

As for those who aren't on the ground or under it, in those vast places that are virtually unknown, there are *massive* numbers of them in the skies, most of the time out of sight of the human eye. There are probably thousands of little ships hovering around, and those quite often are seen, and even occasionally some mid-sized ships.

But there also are huge home ships and operating centers, and it would be a stretch of your imagination to see these mammoth ones. They aren't all that far from Earth, but they are clouded in a sort of preservation atmosphere that's either in the form of clouds, or by using a frequency fluctuator to speed up their vibrational atmosphere, they can stay in hiding when they're practically beside you—well, directly overhead.

....

NO brotherhood members of what are called "alien civilizations" are going to be landing soon! More than likely what will take place is that those already on Earth in either disguise or hiding will emerge first and reduce or take away the fears that might—just *might*—hit the multitudes if thousands of spaceships descended *en masse*.

....

Very likely there will be communication between the ones who are Earth souls, or whatever word is better there—ET folks will do—and those in "space." Obviously coordination will have to take place or it would be a fiasco, and then Earth people *would* get bent out of shape.

....

It's all in readiness as far as the *plans* of the "aliens," but there are many variables connected to Earth. All the folks of space, of origin anywhere, are in place, but not willing to supersede Galactic Federation plans, which are to hold off on a mass arrival. It's the collective mentality on Earth that's the pivotal thing here.

....

There's a communications glitch, but it's in the technology and not the spirit energy. It's not an easy one to fix, but it's sure better to have something mechanical that can be fixed instead of a totally blind mind that *can't* be fixed.

....

There is equipment used to measure distance and frequencies between Earth and a point to be determined by each user. The idea is that if there are spacecraft within the radius of that point in space, you can pull them in with sounds that are "off the wall" rather than within the frequencies operating in Earth's atmosphere.

The concept is good, but the equipment is faulty. You need to discover the causes of the static that's simply giving you false signals. You're not recognizing that or that the data you want is really there, just covered with the static. So, get some clarifying apparatus on that equipment and see if you can strain out the static.

I've been told that you should hear the beeping responses because the troops you're beaming at are homing in on the signals. These are English language or other language-speaking beings, you guys! They know you're trying to communicate in a common language—numbers and frequencies—but it isn't necessary. So, *talk* to them!

But get that static cleared up and then see if you can broadcast a signal. The Morse code would be a good one to send out. We'll see if we can make a contact loop involving the folks here who are set up for monitoring all ET activity relating to Earth.

....

Believe me, you'd *gasp* if you saw how many troops there are and how many souls here are monitoring all the movements! No commanding or coordinating is done from here, just watching, being aware. Some people on Earth are benefiting from this monitoring as some are connected here expressly for this reason.

....

My service at this point is studying the mechanics of taking apart weather anomalies and softening their effects in our atmosphere. And I do mean "our"—like *yours and ours.* We aren't all that far from you, you know, and furthermore, we have such close bonds with you all that we aren't separated in very many ways. By our lighter density and the respective weather, yes, we are, but still it's your AND our atmosphere I'm working on.

I know that sounds almost too weird to believe, but that's the easiest way for me to tell you. That isn't at all how I'd describe it here, but you don't have our words so how could you begin to know what I mean if I use our vocabulary? There aren't any synonyms or similar expressions there for this process. It's something that can't help immediately, but in the long run, what I'm doing will make a good difference.

It's not that I can harness the winds of Earth or act as if I'm a global umbrella in those major storms. I'm studying how to contain the energy so that it can be dispersed rather than congregate and then explode. I should have said dispersed in a routine and slow and easy way instead of just sitting for a while and then acting as if it's got the whole world by the tail and then, watch out—here's another hurricane or tornado!

It's going to take a while for this to have any effect, you know? There's a lot more still to come by whatever designation it's given—cleansing, purification, increasing the light, lightening Earth's burdens of negativity, ascension process—but it all adds up to the very same thing—a lot of geological activity with pretty heavy damage is still in store.

There's no way out of this, you know. Energy is energy, and you can't say, "Shoo, baby, go dissipate." Actually, that's what I'm working on, how to get to that status of being able to handle things so that if rain is needed, it comes, just enough of it. When it's done, it goes away until it's needed again. The rhythm, the pattern is set, you see.

The following excerpts are from Grace's and my conversation last October.

These crews in your skies are getting antsy. They've been ready for *years* to land and get going on the things they can do to help you, that their technologies can.

You've got some developments of your own that have been kept under wraps and a few of you know this and what they're capable of, but just wait until you see ET tech in action!

Also, your weather and "natural" disasters—just a few words about that. You know that for ages much of that has been created by technology combinations controlled by the Illuminati—well, that's going to end in a big hurry. Actually, it's already slowed down a lot, and none of those claims about fantastic—as in fantasy-make believe, not fantastic-fabulous—catastrophic upheavals roving around the Internet will ever happen. Just keep your eye on a glorious world, Earth's Golden Age, and don't be afraid of BIG changes—they're all to the GOOD!

Grace, how are you doing with your "weather of the future"?

Wonderfully! We're all set for the time when Earth has dumped all the negativity and we can act on her choice for a moderate climate everywhere. It won't take as long as you might think to turn deserts into vegetable gardens!

Jeremy

When Jeremy and I talked in 2001, he told me that after receiving advanced training in Nirvana, he had been transferred to another planet in the galaxy where his knowledge and skills were needed.

It is my honor to be given the opportunity to work at this height of light energy that is being strengthened in its velocity toward Earth directly into the oceans. At this time it is required that more light be poured into those waters because there is a need to thwart the most damaging effects of the sonar testing that otherwise would have killed thousands of whales and dolphins as well as other marine life. That testing would have increased ocean waters in temperatures that to human comparison would be past boiling, so you can see that the work we perform in this height and breadth of energy band is critical to preserve that facet of Earth.

I know you have been told the importance of whale spiritual energy that is anchoring on the planet the light forces' energy streamers beamed there. That is true, and that of course is the purpose of my work in tandem with these other souls whose service is the same as mine. We chose to rise into an orbiting pattern within the galaxy that would permit the garnering of light rays from other celestial bodies and direct these beams to Earth.

This in no way deflects the light from serving its full purpose for all other places and life forms, but it permits us to focus the powers of the light instead of having it diffused in space. It is the concentration of energy band that is preserving, to the extent we are able, the health and lives of marine life.

....

Bodies here are not as dense as on Earth and not as light as in Nirvana. My appearance is a male humanoid, I think you'd say most accurately. This body is taller, sturdier and frankly, in the universal view, more handsome than most Earth bodies.

However, the technology inherent in the energy of the lighter density at this level permits materializing any form at will, so I could change this body into whatever shape and size would enable me to perform this service most effectively. I, like those souls working with me, do this quite frequently in aid of collecting the energy streamers and harnessing their power into a direct beam for the most potent absorption by Earth's light workers and from them into the areas of their manifesting focus.

....

My little group is Earth souls on loan to another civilization. We could be considered the visiting advisers, trainers or specialists, and the civilization in which we are living right now could be considered an apprentice army of light workers. Spiritually they are evolved, but technologically they are not, and our purpose here is to teach them what they need to learn about harnessing, directing and intensifying the energy streamers so they are optimally effective. The vantage point of this planet in relationship to Earth provides an ideal channel, or passage, for intensifying the light as it travels from here to Earth. That's why we're here rather than there.

....

We're in the same general area of the galaxy as you are. The light coming into this area from far distant sources could be wasted almost totally if we were not here working along with this benevolent civilization to harness it, bring it into a purposeful use and direction, and see that it is beamed as most needed to Earth. The light we've been sending is not directed only to the oceans, although you could say this is our "passion," but rather dispersed to help achieve balanced energy on the planet.

There is another aspect of our service here, and again, an advantage offered by this placement in relation to the position of Earth. Without us in this position, the abundance of incoming light could be so diffused by the time it reached the other light workers on and around Earth that they would have a much more difficult job performing their specific services.

They are helping the planet maintain regular orbit and helping the natural forces allow milder dispersal of kinetic energy so that it does not require the cataclysmic action that otherwise would be needed. We could be likened to the light gatherers and senders, and the alien civilizations surrounding Earth could be considered the engineers, technicians and hands-on healers. You could call us the way-showers who are beaming light to the dispersers of healing energy on Earth.

....

Part of my agreement—soul contract, if you will—
was to get a good grasp on the feelings, emotions, passions
of and for sea life on the planet as the over-layer of impetus
I needed to qualify me for this higher level energy work.

....

The work of this group I'm with is aimed at
interrupting the dark proclivity that is ordering those
tests to proceed and is legalizing the slaughter of whales
for commercial purposes. So we're working on two fronts.
We're sending the focused intensity to the oceans to
ameliorate the effects of the sonar and other forms of
destruction like sewage, chemical and oil pollution and
over-fishing, as well as directing light energy to the
souls responsible for those acts being carried out.

There are just a few souls who favor this destruction,
but the darkness is firmly entrenched within them and
so we have to work around them. We have to get the
masses of souls within the light so that the quantity of
protests cannot be overcome by those few powerful souls
whose efforts are absolutely engulfed in darkness.

When Jeremy and I talked again last year, I asked if his
group's light-directing service still is needed.

The group was expanded soon after we talked, Suzy.
Matthew and perhaps others as well have told you about
the contingent of dark ones on Earth who refused to join
the light in accordance with their soul-level agreements
and instead, they have continued causing extensive
suffering and destruction. We needed more help to meet
the increased need to harness and direct to Earth the

light beaming in from distant sources.

A tremendous amount of negativity has formed since our first conversation because so much has happened since then—"9/11," war in Iraq and Afghanistan, the Illuminati's weather manipulation and initiation of massive geophysical occurrences, Japan's damaged nuclear plant, the world economy. Dispersing the negativity from all of that and people's reactions has required gargantuan amounts of light, and I can tell you, this has kept those beaming civilizations and us busy nonstop so Earth stays right on target to enter fourth density through that "open astral window" around the end of next year, your time.

....

Due to the tenacity of the dark hearts and minds, a number of extremely serious changes on the planet have to be crammed into little more than a year of your time, and steadily directing to Earth the light from those distant sources will be necessary to ease the months of transition ahead. The more light permeating the people, the less fear they will have about the dramatic differences—not to mention meeting members of various civilizations as they appear in their native lands!

....

From what I've learned in this service and remembered of my other lifetimes with spiritually evolved souls, stick with the light and life just keeps getting better and better!

Ithaca

Ithaca had lived in Nirvana ever since her life ended as a sacrificial virgin during the Inca reign in Peru. That unusually long residency was because she was a highly evolved soul with extraordinary healing abilities. Her energy felt "lilting," like a lullaby, and Matthew said her vibrations are instrumental in helping new arrivals' psyches heal from traumas during the persons' physical lifetimes.

He also explained that because of Ithaca's honored service to the realm, she had been granted her desire to change her Incan sturdiness and coarser features to the petite body, skin tone, fine black shiny hair and delicate features of a young Oriental woman. That's the image she sent to me, and she was wearing an elaborate Oriental dress and sandals.

Ithaca transmitted a great deal of information that became five chapters in *Revelations for a New Era*—the following are excerpts from two chapters.

Before the beginning there was nothing we can know about, and then there happened a great explosion of such intensity that it cannot be imagined. It was the self-expression of Creator Mind, which had existed until that moment silent and motionless. Into the previously unknown came light so intensely brilliant as to be its own radiance.

That moment was the manifestation of Creator's silent idea to share Its total knowledge and power and presence with all subsequent expressions of that original essence. It was not only sharing, it was actually parts of

Creator that came into being in that first moment. Nothing existed before then, and everything that has existed since then has come from Creator, the Source of All That Is.

After Its contemplation to experience through shared life in energy form, Creator first manifested the highest angels. The emergence of that angel life is called First Expression, and those first children of Creator are called the archangels. The essence of Creator was not diminished by creating children, but only shared with them, just as your essence is not diminished by your children, but only shared with them.

In Creator's love for Its children, It gave them free will with its indivisible ability to co-create with Itself whatever manifestations were of the souls' own choosing and ideas. Manifesting at first produced nothing visible except to the Mind of Creator. It was totally a mental process accompanied by what we could call emotional awareness. Simple in theory, it also was simple in the beginning efforts when all consciousness was close to Creator.

Possessing all the powers and capabilities and knowledge of Creator but on a smaller scale, the archangels mastered manifesting instantly because there was no separation of their minds and the Mind of Creator. With Creator, they created the next realm of angels, not quite as high in the light but proportionately still possessing those same elements of knowledge and power as the archangels.

Within those angelic realms there was recognition of the inseparability from Creator and each other because the same creational material was the essence of all. Manifestation was then still only in spirit form, pure energy in love and light. Without division between the Creator and the created, there was only harmony and shared love. That was the original intention of manifestation.

Then, into those stages of cosmic growth came denser formations. Most dense in form were the celestial bodies of the universes and least dense were the beings who went forth as gods or goddesses to rule over them. All of those souls had proportionately the same power, love, knowledge and intent of Creator. One of the gods became the ruler of this universe, and this is the Supreme Being whom many of you call God. Using His co-creative powers with Creator, God became the maker of all life within this universe.

....

The story of Adam and Eve had its roots long before it was recorded as the biblical genesis of human life on Earth. It is a story that has captivated many otherwise searching minds, minds that stopped thinking at that legendary level that defined the development of Earth and its human life.

Without unfolding the layers of mistakes in interpreting universal Beginnings and subsequent occurrences, there can be no truth unfolded, either. It is necessary to unwrap the many untruths so energy alignment can take place for ascending into higher realms of understanding and higher frequencies for spiritual awareness.

Ostensibly, all religions originated their own dogma to benefit the peoples. But in fact, accurate historical recordings show that a few people who wished to control the many peoples deliberately devised falsehoods that enabled this control. Very long ago the religious leaders made up stories to confuse and mislead the minds searching for an understanding of their Beginnings.

The leaders saw that the truth would allow people a closeness to God that did not require money or intervention by other humans, and that did not suit their purposes. So to satisfy their greed and desire for control, the leaders contrived layer upon layer of distance between God and the individual heart and soul. It is their false information that you revere and hold most sacred.

Worshipping God is not kneeling and feeling lowly, it is looking within and exulting in the knowing of one's inseparable God connection. And church is not a building. Church is completely within each soul! The very earliest churches were the only ones in accordance with God's intent.

As explained by your biblical Jesus, when two or three souls gathered to worship in God's name, that was showing glory to Him and therein He would be found. Never was church intended to be a structure, using materials and labors to honor a God increasingly removed from conscious communion. But the diligent and reverent beings who followed the dictates of the self-serving few fell under the spell of the mystery, and soon all truth of one's direct and constant spiritual connection with God diminished almost to extinction.

The deliberate distortion of God's truth is not part of your biblical history, but there is evidence of that fact from records found in caves and tombs. Divinely inspired translations of the ancient languages and depiction of those records were given directly to specially chosen individuals, but those translations have been suppressed by the same dark spirit that was behind the origination of the lies.

....

Those greedy, deceitful Lyran visitors were the originators of some of the later inhabitants of Earth. Their reason for bringing to the planet her original beings was as simple as this, slave labor. The Lyrans felt that for such a purpose no human status with a God connection was necessary, and they brought high-status animals with an instinct for following orders. That introduction of such beings was the beginning of the genetic makeup—the human root stock—of the earliest ancestors of Homo sapiens.

Eventually released from slavery, the embryonic human population flourished in bands in the most habitable lands in the continents now called North and South America and Africa, and in the Middle East regions. Planetary land and sea masses were much different then. As climates changed and as food abundance lessened, the groups migrated to other lands for survival. They developed over many periods, now known as the Pleistocene epoch, some of them called Neanderthal and Cro-Magnon in their evolutionary journey.

At a designated point of evolvement the beings were ready for seeding, which was a mating program to initiate the intelligence and spiritual aspects that would elevate them to fully defined HUMAN status, H(igher) U(niversal) MAN. At the time of the seeding, extraterrestrial humans came to live among the primitive Earth beings. They were from different constellations, thus providing the genes that produced the varieties of body shapes, skin colorings and facial features of current Earth populations. Due to the cohabiting of these extraterrestrials with the Earth population and the direct implantation of intelligence through that genetic structuring, the thinking, reasoning, conscience-endowed Earth humankind came into being.

Theirs was not the ordinary evolutionary process. They were endowed genetically with an intelligence factor that evolved in a time span of only about 30,000 Earth years, a uniquely rapid time in your time structure for any profound development. The DNA containing the intelligence quotient was immediately reproduced in the seeding, thus quickly enhancing development of the Earth human brain.

Thus it can be clearly seen that humankind as represented by Adam and Eve did not spontaneously appear on Earth. Nor did humans descend from the apes as theorized by Darwin. There was a similarity only in ancestral physical form, with approximate sizes and upright movement. All varieties of the ape family on your planet diversified from the original ape root stock. Humankind evolved into current likeness directly from the parallel developing of the human root stock introduced by their extraterrestrial ancestors. The brain and God fragment with soul attachment introduced directly and ONLY into Homo sapiens is the vital difference in the two lineages.

Earth's Golden Age

Foreword

The following is God's and my conversation in 2007 that led to "Essay on 2012." When we reached this part of the book, I told Him I didn't think what we said five years ago needs to be in it.

"Suzy, I want this included. I want my children to know my umbrella God opinion about this matter along with my Matthew-self's information."

During our early talks, which started in 1997, I was still strongly influenced by 35 years of immersion in Christian dogma, and God's explanations about who He is—in brief, an amalgamation of everyone and everything in this universe—were confusing. My asking what He did as our umbrella God amused him, and in our private talks since then, occasionally He refers to Himself that way.

As He added to His original statements, I was feeling uneasy about changing something that had been published. He knew that, of course, and said, *"Calm down, little Suzy, this is for emphasis, and it's my prerogative to do this—it's my book."* So here it is, umbrella God's opinion.

All right, Suzy, let's talk about this topic that's looming larger as the days pass—what's going to happen when you cross off the last days of 2012 on your calendar? The thoughts in many minds about that range from the sublime to the ridiculous, and since the latter is so quickly addressed, that's where I'll begin.

No, your world is not going to end at the end of 2012! Earth is an eternal soul inhabiting a planetary body, and now that it's back from the brink of destruction—

thanks to the infusion of light from your "space" neighbors and those who aren't so close by—and on the way back to its original vibrant health and beauty, she's going to keep it for a long time to come.

And no, she's not going to split herself into two planets, one for good folks and another for the not-so-good ones. Would you split yourself into two pieces, one that works when your conscience does and the other for when you want to tune it out? She's not going to turn upside down either, and none of you is going to be lifted off into a spaceship so you don't fall off when that happens.

Nor are you going to duck for cover by going inside Earth before her surface is obliterated. In returning to her original Eden self, she'll keep all of her beauty spots and restore whatever has been blighted. Another thing, have my children who are happily living inside the planet *invited* you to move in with them?

With "ridiculous" accounted for, what is the "sublime" that you can expect the end of 2012 to bring? Like everything else that happens anywhere, the choice is up to individuals, the decisions each makes.

What I can tell you with certainty is, you who make the trip with Earth into the higher planes will be living in the promised Golden Age. In numerous of his messages, my Matthew-self has accurately described the changes and challenges during the transition between now and your world after 2012 with its astounding differences that you will welcome wholeheartedly.

Suzy, I need your proficiency here, to find all the parts of his messages about this and organize and edit them so the information flows nicely and there's no superfluous or repetitious material. So, will you work with me on this?

Well, of course, if that's what you want. But I'm curious—why you don't just talk about this yourself?

I know all about your curiosity, Suzy. My preference for Matthew's words goes back to this "umbrella God" of yours, the indivisible sum of every single soul in this universe, and to you, that collective multidimensional intelligence is inconceivable.

It is to *everyone* there, and that's my point. I want the information to come from a highly evolved soul whose fairly recent life on Earth and love bonds with some souls living there is a personal perspective as well as an authentic account of Earth's journey into the Golden Age and what life there will be like. I can't think of anyone more appropriate than your dear son, can you?

God, you know perfectly well you're playing up to my maternal genes, don't you!

And why not play my trump card here, "Mother"? I know how much work is involved in what I've asked you to do. After this "Essay on 2012" is in place, I may have a bit more to say besides "Thank you, my beloved child."

Overview

In working together to edit the original essay in accordance with what God wants in this book, Matthew and I eliminated everything that pertained to the transitional stages of ascension—we're already experiencing the situations that the messages forecast. We deleted parts that were more appropriate to place in other sections of this book, and we incorporated relevant information that was transmitted after the essay was completed.

Not all the glories of Earth's Golden Age are awaiting you on the threshold, and once in fourth density, you will not be living in an era of complacent stability. The only constant in the universe is *change!* Not only will marvelous developments continue in all areas of your world, but throughout that magical Age you will keep on growing consciously and spiritually, discovering your innate capabilities to manifest marvels and having adventures that in this moment you cannot even imagine.

It is my joy to tell you what you can look forward to during the years after 2012. Along the way through fourth density, many profound changes worldwide will transform life as you have known it into life in total harmony with all of Nature and thusly flow out into the universe. Anything that happens anywhere affects everything everywhere!

First, as all warring ceases, corrupt leaders are unseated and tyrannical regimes fall, trustworthy individuals with spiritual and moral integrity and expertise in governing will take the helm and bring

order as rapidly as possible. Many wise and able leaders
in previous Earth lifetimes have returned to expand on
their groundwork for this unprecedented time at hand
and others are volunteers from advanced civilizations.

Although money has been the basis for your
commerce, its major use has been to concentrate power
in the hands of a few individuals; therefore, economic
reforms are as crucial as honorable national leadership.
For centuries banking and commerce globally have been
illegally controlled by the Illuminati, a disparate group
of individuals whose greed and corruption through many
generations has produced their vast fortunes and caused
billions to live in impoverishment. This immense
imbalance cannot continue and it won't. Honest,
knowledgeable people will manage the new monetary
system, which will be based on precious metals, and they
will allocate fairly and equitably all of your world's
resources.

Many types of work will change, but everyone who
wants to be employed can be; all salaries and wages will
be equitable and more than sufficient. Greatly enhanced
food production methods will provide an abundance of
nourishment for everyone around the world.

Education at all levels will be accessible and affordable to everyone, and so will attendance at recreational
events—everyone will enjoy more leisure time, which is
so necessary for overall well being. For instance, with
new transportation modes and fair distribution of
wealth, you can comfortably travel worldwide without
any restrictions between countries.

Medical therapies will undergo changes to your
benefit until no procedures of any kind are needed
because bodies will become free of every form of *dis*-ease.

The proliferation of prescription drugs and harmful synthetic "street" drugs will end.

Technologies that have been suppressed by the Illuminati will be brought forth. Those and the advanced technologies of your universal brothers and sisters will eliminate all forms of pollution and harness renewable energy sources. Adaptations will be phased into electrical, electronic and mechanical appliances and systems as photons become as numerous as electrons and then are dominant in Earth's energy field.

Although telepathy will become common, voice-to-voice communication across the miles will be as important as now, and harmful aspects of cell phones, as well as satellite towers, will be eradicated. There will be no more surveillance cameras, wire taps, computer monitoring or any other means whereby your privacy is invaded.

Nuclear power plants will be dismantled and stored nuclear waste dematerialized. As new sources of fuel eliminate your dependence on oil and natural gas, their extraction along with the process called fracking will cease. Oil rigs, utility poles, billboards and anything else that is an eyesore will be removed, and so will expanses of concrete as vehicles that don't need highways become available.

All nations' infrastructures will be soundly built or restored. New types of materials gradually will phase out the need for ore, and land left useless and ugly by mining will be reclaimed and beautified.

Contaminated rivers, lakes and aquifers will be purified, and the use of toxic chemicals will end. Forests, jungles and wetlands will be restored to expand animal habitats and oceans will be returned to health so marine life can flourish. Vast desert areas will become arable and verdant during Earth's restoration to her pristine, beauteous Eden-self.

What you call "El Nino" and "climate change" are Earth's natural processes to return to her original moderate climate worldwide. Glaciers will melt and stark variations in temperatures will diminish until everyplace in your world is comfortably habitable.

Some animals living in the very cold or very hot climates will adapt to the changes and others will migrate, but a few species in Polar Regions will not be able to adjust—by instinct, they will not mate and the species will die out.

Animals in the predator and prey food chain gradually will return to their once peaceable selves, and those that are carnivorous will turn to the plant kingdom for sustenance. Animals that live in the wild will instinctively know when to reproduce so as to maintain a balance with all other species.

While there are countless levels between the lowest and the highest universal intelligence, *no* thing is excluded from the mass consciousness. To be more personal—indeed, to be *more correct*—substitute "soul" for "thing" and you can see the interrelationship of the totality of this universe.

It could be no other way—everything is energy, and the source of all energy is the love-light essence of Creator, the Ultimate Being of the cosmos. In this universe, that same energy is of God, by whatever name one calls the Supreme Being who is our life source.

The higher the vibrations of any environment, the higher are the comprehension capacities of all life within it. Just as you are expanding in consciousness, so is all of Nature growing in varying measures of awareness, and soul-level agreements have been made between humankind and all other life forms.

Although much less lumber will be used than currently, the sacred relationship between trees and humans includes their willingness to be used for decorative parts of building interiors and furniture in the short term, perhaps as long as the next half century.

Plants that were genetically engineered with harmful elements will shed those aspects. Fast-growing food crops, other edible plants and those with medicinal properties will give themselves for your nourishment and health.

Cotton and other fiber-producing plants also have agreed to be used for your needs, and natural construction products like clay, reeds, straw, tropical canes and surface stones are willing to become widely used.

Acknowledgement of all these sources' consciousness and their importance to you and feeling gratitude for their serving your various needs will be inherent in all people. You will come to know and treasure the Devic kingdom, which is so closely allied with the beauty and thriving of all the rest of Nature's realm.

Sonar testing, which is so destructive to marine life, will end. The whales' spiritual mission, to embody in huge bulk in your oceans where they absorb and anchor the light beamed to the planet from distant civilizations, soon will be completed. Whale and dolphin souls will soar to their original high light stations when they leave physically, but they will continue to grace your planet with their love energy.

In accordance with the truths that will be revealed about religious dogmas, only the true spiritual aspects will be retained and the controlling aspects will fall by the wayside.

All unjust, unfair and injurious laws, regulations, policies, practices and cultural customs will be struck down, and negotiating any areas of disagreement will result in satisfying resolutions.

There will be no capital punishment and no need for prisons. Other third density conditions that will disappear include subjugation of women, social caste systems, cruelty to any life form, random violence, mind control, corruption, bureaucratic red tape, wanton destruction, pornography, homelessness, slave trade, media control, and banking and corporate monopolies.

Those and other marvelous differences are indeed momentous changes from life in this moment, yet the greatest transformation of all is YOU! Life will be without fear and divisiveness as peoples of all countries and cultures will be cooperative, innovative, helpful, kind and delightfully good-natured. Hearts and minds will be open, and characteristics like greed, jealousy, envy, prejudice, anger, ruthlessness, superficiality, egotism and dishonesty no longer will be part of anyone's makeup.

As you continue to evolve, the power of your love energy and higher consciousness will enable you to do things that in this moment you would deem miracles. For example, through visualization, you will learn to produce whatever you wish to make.

You will visit persons dear to you who are in Nirvana—visiting was commonplace until third density limitations closed minds to this as even a possibility— and you will communicate telepathically with souls in spirit and in physical civilizations.

You can teleport wherever on Earth you want to go,

perhaps Inner Earth to visit the beautiful souls who live there in phenomenal cities with awe-inspiring facilities. Traveling astrally or in spacecrafts, you will go to see your brothers and sisters in their worlds where energy levels are compatible.

You will *feel* your personal connection with God as you use the innate powers you *always* have had as your birthright, and you will take your rightful place within our universal family of multidimensional, eternal souls.

Earth's Golden Age, where life radiates the love, harmony, serenity, beauty and spiritual awareness that exemplifies the gods and goddesses you are, *already exists in the continuum.* You have achieved what you came to do, and all light beings in this universe honor you and your magnificent co-creation!

More Glimpses of Life Beyond 2012

After "Essay on 2012" was distributed and posted, there was widely expressed interest in specific aspects of life in fourth and fifth density, so they were amplified in subsequent messages.

Health

Along the ascension pathway through fourth density, all physical, emotional and mental disorders will be healed by your lighter bodies' natural mechanisms, and bodies will incrementally re-grow any missing organs, limbs or teeth until every aspect of health is perfected.

Widespread ignorance of bodies' self-healing abilities is a large factor in your current susceptibility to illness and other infirmities, and that is due to ancient civilizations' DNA being "dumbed down" into third density intelligence and spiritual levels by the more powerful dark ones. Along with that serious decrease in comprehension and spiritual awareness, they lowered immune systems so that bodies would be vulnerable to a variety of illnesses and organ deterioration, tampered with brains so that mental diseases could occur, and programmed psyches so that they could be severely traumatized.

In recent times, many other factors have further weakened bodies' resistance to debilitating conditions—laboratory-designed viruses; pollution, including toxins in chemtrails and weaponry; chemicals in prescription drugs, fertilizers and crop pestilence eradication; damaging properties in vaccines; and genetically altered foods. None of those is part of life in fourth density and beyond!

Bodies of aged persons gradually will become youthful and you will live robustly much longer than your current life expectancy. Life spans in fifth density can be tenfold or more than yours are now.

Diet

As you continue your journey into higher vibrations, your bodies' cells will become progressively lighter. Fruits, vegetables and grains will become much more satisfying because they are light-filled foods, and meat and seafood will become less and less appealing until both taste preference and respect for animal life will end the desire to include those in your diet.

Employment

You are accustomed to thinking of employment as a job with salary or wages whereas that word means the use of time, tools or services advantageously—that is what you will be doing in fourth and higher densities. Because many kinds of work that you are accustomed to doing or requiring don't exist in the higher densities, those will be phased out gradually so as not to present hardships to anyone.

Areas that will cease or change considerably include military service and all industries associated with war, chemical production, oil and natural gas extraction, logging, mining and manufacturing.

Multinational corporations and monopolies in any business field have no place in higher densities.

Bodies will be healthy and perfect, so physicians, psychological therapy, pharmaceuticals, prosthetics and health care insurance won't be necessary.

There are no financial binds—no mortgages or other indebtedness—so there is no need for lending institutions, and there is no reason to sue anyone, which eliminates the need for legal counsel in those kinds of matters.

The Federal Reserve System will be abolished along with the IRS, its collection arm in the United States, and for the relatively short time that taxation may exist, it will be fair and the calculating simple, so neither CPAs nor auditors will be necessary for that purpose.

Because many of your laws, regulations and various types of licenses won't be needed, the people who enforce or issue those won't be needed either. There will be far less need for attorneys, judges and court reporters.

You won't miss those kinds of jobs, and you won't miss the common aspects of working. In fourth density there are no tedious, monotonous jobs; no 9:00 a.m. to 5:00 p.m. or weekend workdays or swing-shifts; no long commutes to workplaces or traffic jams; no quotas to fill; and no concerns about loss of jobs.

If your experience and expertise is in a field that is not part of higher density life, please do not fret! Academic studies and training at every level are available to all, and you can choose to enter any field that interests you. The wide variety of possibilities includes communication, education, child care, transportation, clothing design, entertainment, sports, architecture, construction, landscaping, property maintenance, farming, food service, animal care, libraries, artistic and cultural events, publication, commerce and civic administration.

Education

Education will be changing dramatically. In fact, this has begun with the recognition that babies and toddlers have the ability to learn with amazing speed.

Educating youngsters will be easier than *re*educating adults. Very young children haven't been taught inaccurate information, so for them it will be simply learning what *is* accurate. It is possible that some older children and teenagers may be a bit annoyed at first as the new information will render useless much of what they had been taught, but advanced souls born during the past decade or two will revel in being able to go full speed ahead.

Academic systems will stimulate the desire to learn, and preparation and distribution of textbooks along with development of computerized and televised lessons will be done expeditiously. A selection of current books will be preserved as part of Earth's recorded history and the rest will be recycled.

Instruction about accurate planetary history and authentic universal knowledge for every level from early childhood through what you could call post-post-

postdoctoral studies will be available to everyone, and teachers at every level are innately prepared to step into this mission that they chose in pre-birth agreements.

Along with extensive courses in all branches of science, philosophy, mathematics and languages, subjects will include what many now dismiss as "loony New Age thinking"—that is, spiritual and metaphysical—or "wild conspiracies"—such as the truth about many assassinations, corruption in governments and "9/11."

Because all forms of artistic expression come from the soul, music, writing, painting, sculpture and all types of arts and crafts will be given emphasis commensurate with their vital importance.

The greatest change, however, will be the expanded brain usage and increased capacity for reasoning that will lead to much greater interest and facility in acquiring knowledge. This glorious aspect of Earth's Golden Age applies not only to students, but to *everyone* who is living in those high vibrations.

Animals

Beloved animal companions will ascend with their families and so will those animals you consider wild if there are enough years in their soul contracts. Oh indeed, animals have soul contracts—they *are* souls and need to be respected as such!

Their spiritual awareness, sensitivity to energy fluctuations, and extent of emotions and intelligence have been greatly underestimated by most people and completely disregarded by unfeeling humans. Among some animal species, usually those most commonly considered pets, are highly evolved souls who chose to experience in animal bodies, and they have far more wisdom and spiritual clarity than many within your human population.

These animals have come specifically to enhance your relationship with all animal life because this is vital to your individual journeys into the higher vibrations, where cruelty in any form cannot exist. Humans' inhumane treatment and wanton killing of animals throughout the ages contributed in large part to the negativity that caused Earth to drop into deep third density, and her method of releasing negativity is what you call "natural disasters."

Like trees and all the rest of the plant kingdom, animals also made agreements, to provide their bodies for human nourishment. They did *not* agree to living and dying in brutal conditions! Without the dedication of people who are inspired to promote humane conditions or preserve animals' natural habitats, Earth could not have made the progress she has in ascending out of third density.

Animal energy doesn't always embody in animal form, but it can do so for many lifetimes while learning to recognize its value in the Oneness of All. Creator's light essence is the source of all manifested energy, and just as human lives are sacred and inviolate soul-selves, so are the lives of all animals.

Each animal soul goes to Nirvana after its Earth life-time ends and the love bonds that existed between beloved animals and their families reunite them. And, like a human soul, an animal soul chooses its next embodiment based on its past lifetime experiences. As it acquires greater intelligence, it also gains awareness of the inseparability of all life and the direct connection of all with God and Creator.

Eons ago all animals lived peaceably together until the darkness created ferocity in the animal kingdom and developed predator and prey species. That long era is coming to an end, and once again all animals will live peaceably with each other and with humankind and, like you, they will easily and happily adjust to non-meat diets.

Recreation

Just as current employment will be quite different in Earth's Golden Age, so will recreation. It will be what *re-creation* means—time for the spirit to become refreshed, the body rejuvenated.

You will enjoy all the team sports you do now, but without the intensely competitive attitude. Instead of "win at any cost" and "kill 'em" approach to a game, you will play with a spirit of camaraderie and assist each other to develop proficiency. Adjustments to the play itself and protective gear for contact sports will eliminate the likelihood of serious injury; and there is no boxing, which is so destructive to the body. Professional players in every sport will receive reasonable remuneration in keeping with worldwide income fairness.

With respect for all animal life, you won't want to hunt or fish, and there will be no bullfighting or any event that pits animals against each other.

Hikers, campers, mountain climbers, runners, swimmers, divers, boaters, cyclists and para-sailors will have even more beautiful areas to enjoy than now, and there will be archery, target shooting and all winter sports except ice fishing.

With heightened brain usage in the Golden Age, many will be attracted to games and puzzles that are mentally challenging; and reading's former wide appeal, which gave way to television viewing, will make a strong comeback.

Even without today's violence, films in theaters, television programs and handheld games will be just as exciting and interesting. With greater appreciation of all the arts than now, cultural offerings will be popular recreational choices. Attendance cost and accessibility to museums, theatre, concerts, galleries, expositions, sporting events—whatever interests you!—will be easily affordable.

There is no end to what you will find to enjoyably fill leisure time, and you will have considerably more of it than now.

Residences

Architecture will be limited only by imagination, but every building will be attractive and adequate for its purpose. Geodesic domes will be popular and so will fanciful designs that reflect the lightheartedness that so long has been denied the majority of Earth's peoples.

Forms of technology will produce construction materials similar in strength and appearance to tile, concrete, steel, rigid and flexible plastics. Those materials along with natural products and quality simulations of fine woods will be widely used. So will glass, which will be altered from its present breakable composition, because you will desire closeness with Nature even when you are indoors. City life will be much more fulfilling for the spirit than it is today. Substandard buildings will be demolished and once-splendid buildings that fell into decay will be restored. There will be many small parks and colorful playgrounds, vegetable and flower gardens, neighborhood libraries, concerts, museums and galleries with locally produced art forms, and recreational centers for all ages and interests. Animals, even those you now consider wild, will roam freely among all the peoples, and their excrement will not be offensive or problematic.

However, many city dwellers may want to move. Some may prefer to live in farmlands or the solitude and tranquility of rural areas near forests or mountains, and others may choose to live in houseboats on calm seas, rivers or lakes. Still others may decide to live on ocean-going crafts and stay awhile in various foreign ports. And, like a new wave of pioneers, some of you will be inspired to go to currently uninhabitable places when those once again are flourishing.

In short, residence location, style and size will be your choice.

Music

Whether you will be making it, listening to it, or dancing along with it, music will be as uplifting, diverse, thrilling, sing-able, melodic, happily nostalgic or majestic in scope as it is now. What will not make it into the Golden Age are heavy metal instrumentals, lyrics of destructive nature and neoclassical works filled with dissonance—all of those sounds emit much lower frequencies than the vibrations of the Golden Age.

Music in its purest essence is as eternal as the soul and is an inherent ingredient of the energy of love— that's how important music is to ascension and spiritual evolution. The spectrum of benefits from harmonious, melodic tones that flow in intricate beauty from an abundance of fine instruments is limitless, really, because its dominion and healing powers are universal. The angelic realms are in charge, and what a glorious service they perform for all of us!

In higher vibrations tones and colors and aromas blend and waft in a sensory feast that can't be described, only experienced—something to look forward to, no?

Q and A

Among the growing numbers who have heard recently that Earth is ascending, the most frequently asked questions are: *What is ascension all about? How do we prepare for it? Who will go along and who won't, and what will happen to people who won't?*

Ascension

Ascension has nothing whatsoever to do with the "raptures" of religion, so please do not try to fit that concept into the reality. Ascension is the process of Earth leaving third density and traveling through fourth on into fifth.

She is weary of her successive populations' karmic merry-go-round that caused her to spiral downward from fifth density into the depths of third and has kept her there for eons. For her very survival and the lives of all her resident souls, she asked for and received help to ascend out of that low density, where darkness had consigned her for those long ages. She is on her way back to energy planes where only the high vibrations of light prevail, and her humankind whose bodies absorb the light can choose to go with her.

Although this movement is into *planes of successively lighter energy*, not into higher elevations like climbing a stepladder or a mountain, souls' progressive growth in conscious awareness and spiritual clarity can be thought of as upward, thus ascension is the most descriptive term for this advancement.

Some background information will be helpful for understanding why light absorption is essential for physical ascension. In antiquity, strong civilizations with darkness at their core deliberately altered the DNA of weaker civilizations to reduce the people's capacity for intelligence and spiritual awareness. That affected their bodies as well—crystalline cells degraded into the carbon structure that can be, and was, programmed with vulnerability to all forms of illness and depravity as well as a much shorter life span than in eras long, long ago in your concept of time.

The light from other civilizations that saved Earth's very life is restoring the "stolen" DNA in the cells of light-receptive individuals. This not only raises their consciousness levels and renews spiritual clarity, it enables their bodies to survive in the vibrations of the higher energy planes Earth has neared.

Preparation

Absorbing the light that is essential for physically ascending with the planet comes naturally to all who live in godly ways—as God said, *"It is as simple as, BE KIND!"* However, since we have been requested to explain how you can prepare for ascension, we happily offer these additional suggestions.

You think of yourselves as individuals with distinctive personalities, interests, talents, hopes, dreams and accomplishments. That you are, of course, but you are *so much more*, and you need to start thinking of yourselves as inseparable, eternal parts of God and thereby inter-connected with all other life in this universe.

Know that your soul *chose* this lifetime and all of your other lifetimes to experience the fullness of God, and that the goal of every soul is reintegration with God and with Creator, the Ultimate Being of the cosmos and in whom all life had its Beginnings.

Do not fear anything—there is *nothing* to fear! Feel safe wherever you are. When you have completed every-thing you selected in your soul contract, you will move on to your next spirit lifetime and prepare for your next incarnate choices.

Trust and heed your soul's messages to your consciousness—conscience, intuition, instinct, inspiration, aspirations and sense of honor.

Love can be expressed in limitless ways and it must start with the self-love that engenders self-respect, self-worth and self-confidence—with those come humility and thankfulness, not egotism and a sense of superiority.

Live in harmony with Nature. Quiet times in solitude —meditation, if you will—is food for the soul. So is melodic music, which soothes a weary spirit, and the light in a genuine smile has incalculable ripple effects for you and those whose lives you touch.

Be aware of and grateful for the blessings in your life, and don't give your energy to superficial or trivial interests and activities that have no place in fourth density. Instead, direct that energy into avenues that will help you evolve spiritually and consciously.

Cherish beautiful memories and let go of those that are hurtful along with any feelings of resentfulness, bitterness, guilt, prejudice or desire for revenge. All of those negative feelings emit the very low vibrations that don't exist in the Golden Age.

Send love-light to all, especially those in darkness, who are devoid of love, devoid of light, and do not judge others—you don't know your own soul contract, much less anyone else's. Do not hold grudges or feel deeply remorseful—forgive others *and yourself.*

Remember, the universal law of attraction manifests whatever is in your thoughts and feelings. If you are pre-occupied with the individuals and conditions that have caused suffering for many, many souls, you are refueling those attributes and situations. Think instead and act upon what you want in your life and your world: love, joy, fearlessness, harmony, kindness, compassion, mutu-al respect, generosity, helpfulness, cooperation, honesty, forgiveness and thankfulness.

Live from your heart—God also said, *"The heart is the seat of the soul."*

Trust that within your soul is all the information and power you will ever need. Perhaps you will smile when you realize that the enlightenment and guidance we have offered over the years is *your very own knowledge—* all we have done is gently nudge it into your *remembrance.*

Who will ascend and who won't

There is no seat of judgment or arbitrary selection of who may accompany Earth into the Golden Age and who may not—it is strictly a matter of science and each person's conscious choices. Those who choose to live in the light—the ways you could call "godly"—can ascend with Earth, and those who stubbornly cling to their dark ways cannot. After a time in a spirit world that corresponds to their Earth lifetime energy registration, souls in the latter group will incarnate in a world that offers the remedial learning they chose. Divine grace provides each with as many opportunities as necessary to "see the light" and evolve.

Now then, not all light-filled people will go all the way with Earth into fourth density. Again, it depends upon personal choices, and one is the longevity clause in soul contracts. Prior to birth many of today's populace chose to enter spirit life before Earth reaches that wondrous age, and among them are souls whose light is as bright as the noonday sun. Some will depart because they want to see "the big picture" of Earth reaching that milestone in her ascension course.

Individuals who came from highly evolved civilizations to assist Earth in specific ways during her transitional process will have completed their mission, and they may choose to quickly pass through Nirvana to greet souls they know, or they may go to a higher density spirit world, most likely the one serving their homeland. Or, at their evolvement station, they may choose to forego a spirit lifetime and incarnate in another highly advanced civilization for different kinds of growth experiencing.

Souls who completed their third density karmic experiencing will stay for a time in Nirvana, which will remain Earth's spirit world and ascend in tandem with the planet. When they are ready to incarnate, they may choose another Earth lifetime or join a civilization in a different fourth density world.

However, many "good" people will choose to leave rather than believe truthful revelations. People whose rigid religious beliefs are the very foundation of their lives may not be able to accept the truth that religions were devised by the darkly-inclined early heads of church and state to control the masses and garner great wealth. Down through the ages, religious leaders continued to distort the true teachings of God's various emissaries whom He sent to enlighten the people, and all of the falsehoods still are being taught.

Scientists with closed minds also may want to leave when the universal laws are revealed. When those individuals realize that they have devoted their lives to working with flawed concepts, they may opt to transition to a spirit world and prepare for their next physical lifetime with the intention to remember the laws accurately.

And millions may be overwhelmed when the facts about "9/11" and the reasons for current wars—ALL wars!—are disclosed. Veterans in physical and emotional pain and the families and friends of all who died may prefer not to continue living with those truths, which would add to their trauma, and they will leave for the comfort, solace and healing that spirit realms provide.

All of those possible choices are made at *soul level*, they are not conscious decisions, and please do not grieve if persons dearest to you are among them. Spiritual evolvement comes at a pace that is as unique as each soul itself is—when the time is right for your beloved people to consciously accept what in this moment they cannot, they will do so and continue their spiritual growth.

It is natural that you will miss their physical presence, but be heartened by knowing that in most cases, there can be reunions of people in physical worlds with those in spirit worlds even if their densities differ in mass or soul status. Souls who have evolved into a higher density can astrally travel to a lower density that has sufficient light to assure their departure.

Reunions are not possible with souls whose lifetime energy consigned them to first or second density worlds, where intelligence is reduced to instinct and no memories or feelings exist. That primitive state of being is a form of divine grace—it offers those souls a new beginning completely free of cellular memory of the negativity they created that automatically led them to those dense energy levels.

Regardless of the reason a soul leaves this lifetime, physical death will come from any of the many causes that exist now. There will be no mass exodus of persons with dark proclivity when Earth reaches some specific vibratory level because the amount of light within their bodies varies, and many already have died.

There is no way for you to distinguish between light-filled people who have left or soon will depart—whether in accordance with soul contracts or for the other reasons mentioned—and persons whose bodies' viability gets snuffed out because they lack the light to survive in the vibratory level Earth entered.

Because Nirvana is ascending with Earth into the Golden Age, there no longer will be a need to accommodate souls of less than fourth density spiritual status. People whose lifetime choices consign them to lower density realms will go to some other civilization's spirit world that corresponds with their lifetime energy registration. After discovering during their life review process what they need to learn, their next embodiment will be in a density world that offers it.

Some people asked about situations that are personal to them, but their questions and the answers also apply to others.

If someone commits suicide and can't stay in Nirvana since it's going to ascend with the planet into fourth density, what will happen to him?

He may or may not remain in Nirvana. Suicide is not a "sin" as declared by some religions and it doesn't signify that a person's spiritual evolvement status dropped. Although suicide rarely is a soul contract choice, it can be when a loss of that kind is a spiritual growth opportunity for the others who agreed to share the lifetime.

There is no retribution from any source other than possibly self, and self-judgment in the lifeprint review takes into account the entire past lifetime in context of all others. If he had not completed his chosen third density karmic experiencing, his next physical lifetime would be a repeat of the circumstances that will provide a completion opportunity. Like all other souls in Nirvana's third density and lower planes, he will transition to either a spiritual or physical world that corresponds to his lifetime energy.

If he is at a fourth density spiritual status, he may remain in Nirvana or, if he is ready to reincarnate, he may choose another Earth lifetime or embody in another fourth density world for different experiencing.

And, the *only* "sin," if you wish to call an error a sin, is interfering with the growth of a soul, one's own or another's.

What will happen to people who have a mental illness that precludes their making "light" choices?

Mental illness does not preclude persons from

absorbing light.

In cases where the illness is an experience selected in the soul contract, affected persons do absorb light if they adhere to other contract provisions—conscience guides them. If they abide by the conscience and depending upon their contracts' longevity clause, they may ascend and be healed during life in fourth density; if that clause means their time is up imminently, they may petition to amend it for a longer life span. Or they may choose to leave and live in Nirvana until they're ready to incarnate in a healthy body wherever their evolutionary status entitles them.

Individuals who incur diminished mental capacity due to stubbornly behaving in ways that go against the conscience—for instance, excessive indulgence in alcohol and/or illegal drugs—will not have enough light to ascend with Earth. Like all others who ignore soul guidance, those individuals will go to a spirit world that is aligned with their lifetime energy.

There is another factor here. Some persons who commit acts of violence, sometimes causing a shocking number of deaths and injuries, may be adjudged insane, but actually they were acting under mind control. Never is mind control part of any soul contract, nor is the programming done by consent, and those individuals do not incur harsh karma from their actions. Like every other person, it is the lifetime energy registration that determines the amount of light absorbed.

Neither any mental illness nor mind control exists in spirit worlds or physical worlds of fourth or higher density.

Is it possible for people in prison to get enough light

to go forward with Earth?

Absolutely it is possible—and there are no prisons or prisoners in Earth's Golden Age!

Each case is as unique as the person is, and both the crime and the incarceration may or may not be part of the soul contract. This also applies to all former prisoners who served their full sentences or are on parole.

If the criminal acts and the consequences are what the individuals chose to complete third density karmic lessons and balance other lifetimes, those who fulfill that experiencing in accordance with their contracts evolve spiritually. They can travel with Earth into fourth density if the longevity chosen in their contracts permits. If it doesn't, they can petition to amend that clause and physically ascend or they can choose to enter Nirvana with fourth density spiritual status.

Prisoners who don't adhere to their contracts during confinement—that is, their thoughts and actions are steeped in negativity—cannot absorb the light that is necessary for ascending into fourth density. They will transition to a spirit world where learning opportunities are in accordance with their needs.

People who were imprisoned because they ignored the guidance of their conscience and seriously veered from their soul contracts also will leave and go to a spirit realm that offers the learning they require.

Individuals who have been falsely accused and wrongfully imprisoned can take leaps in soul growth if they retain or absorb light throughout incarceration. They also have the option to petition their soul contract's longevity clause, if need be, to physically ascend or they can choose to enter Nirvana in accordance with their original choice time-wise.

Can a drug addict go along with Earth?

The addiction itself will not prevent a person from physical ascension. Although drugs are a barrier to light entering a body, persons who are living in godly ways otherwise do absorb a degree of light; and if they are making a genuine attempt to overcome their addictive nature, they will benefit from the prevailing higher frequencies that are magnifying positive attitudes.

Each case is dependent upon adherence to the soul contract insofar as chosen lessons and age span. If those conditions are met, an addictive nature, like all other infirmities, will be healed along Earth's ascension pathway.

Individuals who don't desire to stop their use of drugs or any addictive behavior and do whatever is necessary to support their habits, will not have enough light to physically survive in fourth density's high vibrations. They will go to a spirit world commensurate with their lifetime energy, where they will have an opportunity to grow consciously and spiritually so their next physical experience can be fulfilling without any addictions.

To get to the Golden Age, do I have to stop eating meat or only eat organically?

While we honor all who choose to be vegetarians or vegans, those diets are not a requirement for ascension. Each person's body is as different as each soul, and at this point, some bodies thrive without meat while others do not. Pay attention to your bodies—they will tell you what they need for maximum well being.

"Eating organically" may be healthier, but it is not a necessity for ascension either. And if the higher cost of organic products presents a financial hardship, don't buy it—the negativity of stress is far more harmful than eating non-organically grown foods. Simply eat sensibly and use the power of thought—*what you are eating serves your highest good*—and feel grateful for the food.

Be heartened by knowing that it won't be too long before all foods will be pure, free of harmful chemicals and genetic alterations.

Various readers have asked if enjoying pornography, gambling, sex parties, extramarital relationships or "dabbling in black magic" will prevent physical ascension with Earth.

It can, because those activities generate the very low vibrations that cannot enter the high vibratory planes of fourth density; however, like every other kind of behavior, it depends upon the experiencing chosen in soul contracts to balance other lifetimes. None of those forms of diversion exists in the Golden Age.

Adults can understand how to prepare for ascension, but babies and toddlers can't. Will they ascend easily without that, and how can parents prepare older children?

Many souls chose very brief lifetimes to benefit themselves and all others in the pre-birth agreements, and their life spans will be too short for physical ascension.

Souls who came in recently with contracts that include lifetimes extending beyond 2012 will ascend with ease. Some infants are born with the crystalline cellular structure that gives spiritual clarity, so many youngsters consciously know their God connection and their rightful place in our universal family.

However, even children without that advantage will experience much less upsetting physical and emotional symptoms than adults whose bodies are changing from carbon-based cells to crystalline. Part of adults' adjustment process is the uprooting and discarding of thought patterns that form belief systems and behavior patterns that are retained in cellular memory. Because young children simply have not lived long enough to have those memories reinforced, they respond more quickly and positively to the higher vibrations than adults.

As for preparing children who are older, do it by example. Live fearlessly, be honest, express your thankfulness for the blessings in your life and the beauties of Earth, and share generously with persons in need.

Keep your mind open to new perspectives and be discerning in your decisions. Be resilient, learn from failure, make the effort again. Dump emotional garbage and superficial interests. Laugh and smile often.

Listen to the children. Ask the older ones to talk about their ideas, fears, plans, hopes, dreams, disappointments. Encourage them to set realistic but not limiting goals and to emulate but not compare themselves with individuals who inspire them.

Let your life exemplify to your children the power of unconditional love for all of humanity and all of Nature.

How can we help our children clear their karma so

they can move into fourth density and beyond?

Children who have not been programmed by "authority figures" act upon instinct and intuition, which is in consonance with their soul contracts, and the "clearing of karma" naturally follows. It is adults who devise unnecessary complexities for themselves by overly analyzing and calculating the very things that children automatically do so simply.

If your older children have been oriented to believe what they have been told by individuals who are considered to be experts or authorities, it will be helpful for the children if you discuss with them the aforementioned suggestions. It would be wise to avoid overwhelming them with information—offer it in stages and encourage them to speak about their reactions.

I've tried and tried to discover my life's mission and I'm afraid that I won't know what it is in time to go with Earth into her Golden Age.

Knowing your life's mission is *not* a prerequisite for entering the Golden Age!

Every one of you is important or you wouldn't be where you are. You don't remember that not only did you choose to live during this unprecedented time in the universe, but you were *selected* because of your collective lifetime experience, wisdom and spiritual strength.

Even lightworkers with many lifetimes of experience in the vital fields where they are holding influential positions don't realize that doing so is the mission they chose in their soul contracts. Because relatively few are needed in leadership capacities, the rest of you are the support team members that are so essential.

Some special roles aren't evident because the need is yet to come. When that moment arrives, you will intuitively know how to proceed. However, in most cases, you are fulfilling your chosen mission simply by BEing the light that you ARE. Don't ever underestimate the power generated by one person's light!

The more evolved a soul is, the more inspired it is to help others. The unified purpose of some civilizations in higher densities is beaming their intense light to lower-density populations to help them progress, and some of you came from those civilizations specifically to radiate your light to benefit less evolved souls on Earth.

If I'm having trouble seeing myself or anyone else as a god or goddess, will this reduce my chances of ascending with Earth?

Anyone whose self-identity is based on wanting to feel "god-like" is looking outside instead of *knowing* inside. According to the gender each of you chose for this lifetime, you are designated as either a god or a goddess, but that differentiation is not important—knowing that every one of you is a part of God IS! God is androgynous, the balance of feminine and masculine *energies,* and those have nothing at all to do with gender, but with *soul essence.*

It could be helpful and equally accurate to think of humanity as that essence instead of individual gods or goddesses, which only signifies the gender choice of each soul for this lifetime. Because this could give rise to questions about bisexual and transgender persons, I repeat that it is *essence*—not form and features or sexuality or gender—that constitutes a soul.

It is the choices each of you makes in using your essence that results in living in "god-like" ways or not. Everything in our universe is eternally interconnected with and inseparable from God, by whatever name you call Him, and every soul is a part of that Oneness.

Can gays and lesbians ascend with the planet?

Indeed they can, but like everyone else, it depends on how closely they have adhered to their soul contracts and the life span they chose in the contracts.

Homosexuality isn't understood on Earth as the advancement in soul evolvement that it is. As a soul grows spiritually and intellectually, eventually it starts integrating feminine and masculine energies—you call that homosexuality.

Just as masculine energy is not the province of only male individuals, feminine energy is not confined to females. The goal of *every* soul is androgyny, the ideal balance of those two energies.

Our "future" already is set in the continuum, so it's known how many people on the planet will make it to the Golden Age, right?

No, it isn't known how many souls will accompany Earth because of all the variables that can affect the final count—provisions of original soul contracts, uncompleted contracts, amended contracts, free will choices that affect only oneself and the choices that profoundly affect many others.

The continuum comprises every single thought form

that has come into existence since the occurrence of what you call "the big bang." Depending upon the amount of energy put into each thought form, every situation is a possibility, probability or certainty, and those potentialities change by the nanosecond. When you put every person on the planet into that context, you can see why it won't be known how many will accompany Earth until "after the fact."

Will the death of so many individuals who don't ascend with Earth cause turmoil and grief that will be a destabilizing influence on the planet?

The numbers of souls who won't physically ascend with Earth cannot be forecast, but those who don't because they refused the light will greatly *lessen* turmoil—they are the ones who fomented most of it!— and their departure will have a stabilizing effect on the planet.

All who accompany Earth into the higher densities have absorbed the light—that's why they could make the trip—that enhances spiritual understanding. Because they know that love bonds are as eternal as the soul itself and they will be reunited with their dearest persons, they won't have intense or prolonged grief about those who moved on to spirit lifetimes.

What is sex like in 5th density?

The answer depends on whether the lifetime is in a physical civilization or a spirit realm, and even when those two residences are further defined, there is no uniform description.

Some physical civilizations have advanced to fifth density intellectually but they haven't a shred of spirituality, and their sexual practices are as brutal as the peoples' nature.

Some civilizations that are spiritually advanced to fifth density or beyond choose bodies of lower density mass so they can experience the closeness of sexual relations and birth instead of employing other means of reproduction such as cloning or intently focused thought. Residents of *all* spirit realms regardless of density have no reproductive organs, so sex as you know it doesn't exist.

What you can anticipate when Earth reaches her destination in fifth density is, all sexual unions will be blissful with mutually sublime sensations for the partners.

But we are happy to assure you, the joy of lovemaking in *fourth* density is not to be sneezed at!

How will justice be served if the dark ones die before they're convicted for their crimes? If they've been cloned, will their clones go on trial in the Golden Age? If so, how will we know if it's a real person or a clone?

Some persons in the dark camp have died, and prior to Earth's entry into fourth density, the rest of them will, so time is the major factor here.

Some persons may live long enough to be prosecuted for their criminal acts, but considering that little time remains before the vibrations are too high for their bodies to survive, it is likely that most will not. If a cloned person has died and clones carried on, the laws will apply to the last clone because continuing the person's illegal or ungodly ways was the purpose of cloning—in time, the fact that certain persons were cloned for that purpose will be revealed.

However, the effective duration of a clone depends on the soundness of the person's mind and body when the first clone was made and how many were subsequently produced. Each clone after the first degenerates to some degree and that requires increasingly frequent replacements. That is another factor insofar as standing trial—the final clone may not last long enough to enter your justice system.

Even if all the individuals who have committed crimes against humanity and perpetrated other deeds that adversely affected life on Earth did live long enough to face arrest, trial or conviction within your year 2012, they couldn't be incarcerated very long because their bodies don't have enough light to survive in the higher frequencies of the Golden Age.

However, their identities will become part of your world's history and not one will escape self-judgment. By the laws of physics in this universe, throughout the life review process in a spirit world where their lifetime energy automatically draws them, they will feel exactly the same pain and anguish as did all those whose lives their diabolical deeds affected. This excruciating self-punishment process is beyond your capacity to imagine, and so is those individuals' *de*volved capacity in their next incarnation.

Knowing what lies ahead for them and understanding that they are the weakest links in the eternal chain that is our soul family will let you more easily feel forgiveness. The high vibrations of forgiveness, like all other godly expressions, are soul growth in action and have a positive effect on the entire universe.

Will there be any need in the Golden Age for a government as we now know it?

Certainly not the types of governments you know, most of which have been corrupt or tyrannical!

A governing system at levels from community to international to multidimensional will serve for communication, coordination and cooperation. Among the welcome changes from current governments will be the moral and spiritual character, wisdom and vision of the leaders; extent of jurisdictions; judicious use of authority; fair and honest legal and justice systems and election procedures—and the approval and satisfaction of all the governed people!

If there's a globally moderate temperature in higher densities, does this mean no more snowcapped mountains?

Goodness no! That would also mean little variance in topography, and most assuredly your Himalayas, Alps, Andes and Rocky Mountains will not be leveled!

The current extremes of burning deserts and sub-zero climes gradually will moderate within a comfortable temperature range, but the awe-inspiring scenery of snowcapped mountains will not disappear. Their beauty is one of the desirable aspects of life on Earth, and skiers, snowboarders and mountain climbers will continue to enjoy those activities.

You've said that heeding intuition is important for making the journey with Earth to her Golden Age. How can we know what is intuition and what is our own thoughts?

Intuition is an instantaneous reaction to a new situation or new information and is a sensation more than a "full blown" thought. What you call a "fleeting thought" may be intuition, but if your impression of the situation or information comes after a pause and has clear mental focus, then it is a thought. Pondering or analyzing any issue is your own thoughts about it.

You could think of intuition as the signal that motivates you to take instant action in accordance with your spontaneous reflex or to seriously think about why you had the reaction you did—perhaps a lifesaving measure or a job change, respectively.

How does it feel to be in fourth and fifth densities?

Describing something that is so much more glorious than any experience you have had in this lifetime can only be a feeble effort compared to the reality, but I shall try.

Imagine feeling such abundant happiness and love that you think your heart will burst. Imagine living so vibrantly that you glow like the sun itself. Imagine embracing souls in spirit who are most dear to you. Imagine traveling among the stars to other worlds, meeting people who seem magical, communicating with the speed of a thought, and performing feats that now you would call miracles.

That may give you a wee glimmer of the magnificence awaiting you in Earth's Golden Age.

Postlude

Now that you have become acquainted with some of my other children—your brothers and sisters—wouldn't you say that we're a pretty inspirational family?

You know more about yourself, too. You know that you are an inviolate, independent, eternal soul as well as an inseparable part of me and of all other life in our universe.

It's an ideal arrangement that keeps getting better and better—you'll see this for yourself in Earth's Golden Age. What a grand adventure we'll have!

Like my child Gaia, I am overflowing with joy and excitement that she is going home and you're going with her.

Well done, my beloveds!

My infinite, unconditional love for you is expressed *by* you and *through* you.

We are ONE.

OTHER MATTHEW BOOKS

Matthew, Tell Me about Heaven
A Firsthand Description of the Afterlife

Life in the spirit world we call Heaven is
active, vibrant and temporary. Matthew
describes the reception of arriving souls,
environment, relationships, communication, animals, reunions, nourishment,
recreation, education, cultural resources,
employment, pre-birth agreements, karma,
past-life reviews, and preparation for our
next physical lifetime.

**Matthew Ward
1962-1980**

Revelations for a New Era
Keys to Restoring Paradise on Earth

Through this book we can learn about our souls, the order
of the universe and how thoughts create everything within it,
the origin of human life on Earth and human cloning here, and
who the reptilians are. Views from Nirvana of our controversial
issues show the great difference in the two perspectives, and
representatives of civilizations far advanced from ours tell
about life in their homelands. September 2001 messages reveal
what happened on "9/11" and in the aftermath.

Illuminations for a New Era
Understanding These Turbulent Times

God's descriptions of who He is give us more insight into
who we are and the purpose of our multiple lifetimes. To help
us understand what is happening in our world, topics of timely
importance include Earth's ascension, why there will be no
nuclear war, reasons for the invasion of Iraq, how we create our
reality, media control, what love is and its power in our lives.
More messages from other civilizations and more glimpses of

life in Nirvana through Matthew's evolution provide further awareness about past, present and future in our linear time.

Voices of the Universe
Your Voice Affects the Universe: Let It Be with LOVE

The voices of God, Earth souls in spirit, members of our universal family and some of our own show the interconnectedness of All. Synchronicity in life experiences and the influence of the Illuminati give insight into this unprecedented time on our planet as Earth is restored to her Eden self, the Golden Age, and our roles in this transformation.

Amusing to Profound
My Conversations with Animals I and II
Suzanne Ward

What the animals in this book talk about shows that the range and depth of intelligence, emotions and comprehension in Earth's animal kingdom far exceeds what usually is attributed to any life except human. These animals' comments—at times, with astounding knowledge and perception—will evoke smiles, amazement, and maybe heartwarming memories or a tear or two.

Order these books at **www.matthewbooks.com** or your favorite local or on-line bookstore.

Messages
Matthew's messages from December 2003 to date are posted on **www.matthewbooks.com**. Topics include current events in a universal context, the ongoing spiritual renewal and world transformation, effects of planetary cleansing and Earth's ascension into higher vibrations, and what we can expect during the transitional period through 2012 and beyond, the era of the Golden Age. Translations of the messages into 23 languages are posted at **www.galacticchannelings.com**.